P9-BZB-575

William Faulkner

The Making of a Novelist

William Faulkner
The Making of a Novelist

Martin Kreiswirth

The University of Georgia Press
Athens

Copyright © 1983 by the University of Georgia Press
Athens, Georgia 30602
All rights reserved

Designed by Kathi L. Dailey
Set in 11 on 13 Times Roman

The paper in this book meets the guidelines for permanence and
durability of the Committee on Production Guidelines for Book
Longevity of the Council on Library Resources.

Printed in the United States of America

Library of Congress Cataloging in Publication Data

Kreiswirth, Martin.
    William Faulkner, the making of a novelist.

    Includes bibliographical references and index.
    1. Faulkner, William, 1897–1962—Criticism and interpretation.
I. Title.
PS3511.A86Z873 1983   813′.52   83-1354
ISBN 0-8203-0672-X

For my parents,
Allen and Pearl Kreiswirth,
and for Kinny

Contents

Acknowledgments

I gratefully acknowledge the financial support provided by the Canada Council, the University of Toronto, and the University of Western Ontario at different stages during the preparation and writing of this book. I am also grateful to the Henry W. and Albert A. Berg and Arents Collections of the New York Public Library, Astor, Lenox, and Tilden Foundations, for giving me access to the Faulkner materials in their possession and to Mrs. Jill Faulkner Summers for permission to quote from unpublished manuscripts. Brief portions of chapters 1 and 2 and a section of chapter 6 originally appeared in, respectively, "The Will to Create: Faulkner's Apprenticeship and Willard Huntington Wright," *Arizona Quarterly* 37 (1981): 149–65, and "Learning as He Wrote: Re-Used Materials in *The Sound and the Fury*," *Mississippi Quarterly* 34 (1981): 291–98.

My thanks are particularly due to Mrs. Freda Gough for her most efficient typing, to Professor Thomas L. McHaney, Professor T. H. Adamowski, and Avrum Fenson for their close and extremely helpful readings of the typescript, to Professor Michael Millgate both for his encouragement and criticism of my work and for the scholarly example set by his own, and, above all, to my wife, Kinny, for all her patience and support.

Abbreviations

Works by William Faulkner frequently cited in the text and in the notes have been identified by the following abbreviations:

EP *William Faulkner: Early Prose and Poetry.* Compilation and Introduction by Carvel Collins. Boston: Little, Brown, 1962.

FD *Flags in the Dust.* Edited by Douglas Day. New York: Random House, 1973.

FU *Faulkner in the University: Class Conferences at the University of Virginia, 1957–1958.* Edited by Frederick L. Gwynn and Joseph L. Blotner. Charlottesville: University Press of Virginia, 1977.

GB *A Green Bough.* New York: Smith and Haas, 1933.

L *Selected Letters of William Faulkner.* Edited by Joseph Blotner. New York: Random House, 1977.

LG *Lion in the Garden: Interviews with William Faulkner, 1926–1962.* Edited by James B. Meriwether and Michael Millgate. New York: Random House, 1968.

M *Mosquitoes.* New York: Liveright, 1951.

MF *The Marble Faun.* Boston: Four Seas, 1924.

NO *William Faulkner: New Orleans Sketches.* Edited by Carvel Collins. New York: Random House, 1968.

SF *The Sound and the Fury.* New York: Random House, 1966.

SP *Soldiers' Pay.* New York: Liveright, 1951.

1.
The Will to Create
Poetry and Imitation

When, in 1928, William Faulkner closed his doors to publishers—or so he later declared—and began writing *The Sound and the Fury* only for himself, it seemed as if he were beginning his literary career anew. For him that novel was a decisive turning point, unique in its conception, composition, and execution. Critics, too, have insisted almost unanimously on the singularity of this first and perhaps greatest of his major achievements, emphasizing the degree to which it differed in substance, technique, and accomplishment from the works that preceded it. *The Sound and the Fury* appears, in fact, to mark an almost seismic break with Faulkner's literary past, a quantum leap in his imaginative development; it is as if the earlier works belonged to another writer—"Faulkner before Faulkner," as André Bleikasten puts it[1]—and as if *The Sound and the Fury* alone transformed "Faulkner" into what Michel Foucault calls "the name of the author" and accorded it the attendant cultural and linguistic privileges.[2]

Bleikasten, in his fine discussion of the early career, sees Faulkner's development as "a series of discrete creative moments, each of which was a fresh start and a new risk," and

Faulkner himself as "a restless experimentalist, an inde-
fatigable rebeginner . . . a writer of many births."[3] Yet although Bleikasten traces "many constants and continuities"
between *The Sound and the Fury* and what came before it,
he leaves no doubt as to when the true moment of parturition
occurred: "It was a sudden leap, unforeseen and unforesee-
able. Hints may be found in Faulkner's early work of what
he was to achieve in *The Sound and the Fury* and in his
other major novels. Yet they are promises only for having
been kept. Faulkner's early poetry and prose are evidence
of immature talent and nothing more. Between them and his
first masterpiece there is all the inexplicable distance from
talent to genius."[4] The creation of *The Sound and the Fury*
must indeed remain inexplicable and mysterious, as Bleikasten and others insist. It did mark an astonishing advance
in Faulkner's work, and any attempt to identify the sources
of a major work of art must in any case be regarded as
highly problematical. Even so, it can be argued that *The
Sound and Fury* was not, to use Bleikasten's terms, Faulkner's first "fresh start" or "new risk," and that our under-
standing of it and of Faulkner's career as a whole may be
enhanced—the mystery not solved but perhaps delimited—
by the exercise of setting this fourth novel as squarely as
possible within the context of his earlier work.

    In fact, *The Sound and the Fury* is more intimately related
to its Faulknerian antecedents than has been formerly thought.
Its very uniqueness depends to a remarkable degree on the
transmutation of themes, narrative strategies, and actual
scenes from those earlier texts. Rather than an absolute
break or recoil from his past, *The Sound and the Fury* represents a moment of "initiation" in which Faulkner learned
"freshly to read himself" and to shape his future in response
to that reading.[5] With this text Faulkner found what Faulkner had been from the beginning. Underlying the strikingly
obvious technical differences between *The Sound and the*

Fury and its predecessors is a fundamental similarity in creative procedure, a common reliance on the exploration of new forms in combination with the reworking of previously exploited literary materials. If *The Sound and the Fury* is a creative leap, the early works not only provided Faulkner with a solid base to leap from but also the skill and self-confidence to make such a leap successful.

Although critics have tended to view Faulkner's career up to *The Sound and the Fury* as "a chartless voyage" or "unpredictable adventure," the process by which he became a novelist capable of this book's achievement was in fact a very gradual and deliberate one.[6] His apprenticeship was long and, in many ways, difficult. From the first stirrings of the literary impulse, Faulkner later stated, he self-consciously set out to learn all he could about the craft of writing (*L*, p. 338). His education, like that of many other writers—perhaps, in some sense, of all other writers—consisted essentially of reading widely in speculative and imaginative works. Every serious writer comes to literature from literature and is therefore caught, as soon as he picks up his pen, in what has been aptly called the "originality paradox."[7] He realizes that he must invent something perceived as "new"; he sees no less clearly that art, in essence, can never be new but is necessarily built on its own past.[8] This primal dilemma is as old as art itself and has gathered around it a rich and diverse body of critical thought.[9] The problem, nevertheless, remains insoluble, and the artist is inevitably trapped in its double bind. The neophyte, of course, feels the pressure most acutely, and whether the paradox is ultimately experienced as an anxiety or as a tension, he must come pragmatically to terms with it before he can create.[10] A standard response to the dilemma was formulated early: at least since the time of Longinus young artists have been told to imitate the works of their predecessors in the hope of assimilating expressive conventions.[11] Later, when originality became a standard criterion of aesthetic evaluation, discipleship was seen as a way of allowing the artist to participate directly in the traditions of the past at the same time as he was developing his own distinctive powers.

This process of imitative apprenticeship obviously takes different forms in different artists. Faulkner's case, however, seems in certain respects to be rather extreme—in terms of the quantity of exploratory work and of the duration of the training period. As critics have repeatedly pointed out, practically all of Faulkner's poetry—his first verbal medium—is in some sense derivative. And it has been by now clearly shown that particular poems are modeled on, or extensively borrowed from, existing poems by Algernon Charles Swinburne, A. E. Housman, T. S. Eliot, Ezra Pound, Paul Verlaine, and minor figures such as Arthur Symons and Robert Nichols.[12] What has not been so fully appreciated is the extent to which this fundamental derivativeness, far from being accidental or deceitful, represents an attempt on Faulkner's part to follow through a deliberate program of apprenticeship involving discipleship, imitation, and even a kind of outright duplication that approaches plagiarism.

Although Faulkner could have picked up the notion of literary apprenticeship from many sources, Phil Stone, his most sympathetic supporter and advisor during this period, encouraged its adoption as a practical course of education: "Try writing in somebody else's style. . . . Then compare yours with his and see how much better he does it. Read a poem until you think you are familiar with it and shut the book and try to write it."[13] Stone's writings establish that he based this advice specifically on the methods advocated in Willard Huntington Wright's *The Creative Will: Studies in the Philosophy and the Syntax of Aesthetics*, first published in 1916. To disregard Wright's importance for Faulkner, said Stone in 1931, would be "a serious omission because the aesthetics theories set forth in that book, strained through my own mind, constitutes [sic] one of the most important influences in Bill's whole literary career. If people who read him would simply read Wright's book they would see what he is driving at from a literary standpoint."[14] Prompted by Stone, Faulkner evidently read *The Creative Will* with care, finding in it articulations of aesthetic propositions, technical theories, and even methodological procedures that he would invoke, explicitly and implicitly, throughout his subsequent career.[15] Since many of Wright's propositions were themselves derived from earlier sources—his position on regionalism, for example, seems to have been based on a famous observation of Hippolyte Taine's—it is often difficult to determine just how much Faulkner took directly from him.[16] But there is little doubt that Wright, as read by Faulkner and reinforced by Stone, was the principal source of those strategies of creative self-development that played such an important part in the shaping of Faulkner's early work.

Central to Wright's theories was the concept of progressive aesthetic evolution through time, and although he did not explore the psychocreative effects of artistic heritage, his discussion of the relation between past achievement and present production was extremely wide-ranging and pursued through a variety of contexts. Wright's dictum that the "entire past progress of an art is condensed and expressed in each of its great exponents" may seem extreme, but it constituted for Faulkner a necessary corrective to some of the self-consciously "modern" movements—"the pack belling loudly after contemporary poets" (*EP*, p. 116)—that had adopted a fundamentally ahistorical aesthetic and attempted "to create the illusion of force by frenzy and motion" (*EP*, p. 117). Wright asserted that the "past is a very necessary foundation on which to build the structure of contemporary art"; since he also believed that "every genuine innovation of method must be developed and consummated before a new one can take its place," his advice for beginning artists necessarily involved the direct assimilation of these "methods" by the examination and imitation of existing works of art. "Every man of genius," Wright declared, "has at some early period played the plagiarist to more than one master," for those artists "who imitate consciously are actively weighing the achievement of the centuries in the scales of analytic intelligence for the purpose of making a temperamental choice of method." "Discipledom in the young artist," Wright explained further, "is as necessary as his later emancipation. No one can commence building an art where his most advanced predecessor left off. He must travel the same road as that taken by his predecessor if he is ever to outdistance him." And he continued: "Every artist who eventually achieves greatness passes at some time in his early development through a period of sedulous eclecticism; and his future is determined by his thoroughness during this hazardous period and by the intelligent manner in which he incorporates into his own art the solutions of problems relative to himself. In the serious and genuine artist this impulse toward imitation grows out of a need for self-revelation: he increases his power, and at last discovers his individual destiny."[17] Wright's appeal for Faulkner as a beginning artist lay precisely in the stress he placed on the utility rather than the anxiety of influence, his tendency to emphasize the necessity of discipleship and downplay the paradoxes of invention. So, many years later, Faulkner himself would advise young writers to engage in a similar program: "Read everything—trash, classics, good and bad, and see how they do it. Just like a carpenter who works as an apprentice and studies the master" (*LG*, p. 55).

One of the most significant, and perhaps the first, of the writers whom Faulkner studied was Swinburne, whose poetry not only provided him with what he called "a flexible vessel" into which he could put his "own vague emotional shapes" (*EP*, p. 114) but also supplied him with concrete

models for poetic exercises. Whereas Faulkner freely borrowed from the first chorus of *Atalanta in Calydon* and from
"In the Orchard" for much of the diction and imagery of a
number of his early poems, his program of apprenticeship
is most clearly visible in his detailed reworkings of "Sapphics" and "Hermaphroditus."[18] Critics have been too will-
ing to accuse Faulkner of merely plagiarizing Swinburne's
poems;[19] a comparison of the imitations and the originals
reveals that Faulkner's versions function more like adaptations or translations than unabashed duplications. In
"Sapphics," for example, while retaining the dominant imagery and certain syntactical structures, Faulkner drastically
condensed Swinburne's twenty stanzas into six, as if he had
deliberately set out to discover what in the model poem was
absolutely essential. Faulkner's version thus appears to be
a study in poetic compression and concision, a conscious
literary exercise—precisely the kind suggested by Wright—
rather than an unthinking imitation or independent imaginative act. Swinburne's poem provided him with a formal
configuration that focused and directed his own poetic experimentation, posing problems for solution that were, as
Wright stated, "relative to himself."

Faulkner's "Hermaphroditus" offers an even more revealing instance of this kind of literary exercise, and a comparison of it with Swinburne's original not only further
demonstrates the educational process in which Faulkner was
then engaged, but also serves to isolate those technical and
artistic decisions that can be seen indubitably as Faulkner's
own. His re-creation of "Hermaphroditus," like his version
of "Sapphics," primarily involves a compression of the prototype's formal structure. Whereas Swinburne's poem is
constructed of four numbered Italian sonnets, each contrib-
uting to an elaborately developed vision that exploits the
sexual and psychological ambiguities implicit in the Hermaphroditus myth, Faulkner's version, published as Poem

XXXVIII of *A Green Bough* and entitled "Hermaphroditus"
in typescript, is a single modified Italian sonnet centered on
an image from Swinburne's first stanza: "Of all things tired
thy lips look weariest, / Save the long smile that they are
wearied of."[20] Faulkner employs this image as a metaphor
for the Hermaphroditic condition, emphasizing the tension
between the secret and unique sexual knowledge on the one
hand and the unnatural and sterile consequences of that
knowledge on the other:

> Lips that of thy weary all seem weariest,
> And wearier for the curled and pallid sly
> Still riddle of thy secret face, and thy
> Sick despair of its own ill obsessed;
> Lay no hand to heart, do not protest
> That smiling leaves thy tired mouth reconciled,
> For swearing so keeps thee but ill beguiled
> With secret joy of thine own flank and breast.   [*GB*, p. 61]

In another version of this sonnet, published in *Mosquitoes*,
line five reads "Lay not to heart thy boy's hand, to protest,"
and "woman's" appears instead of "flank and" in line eight
(*M*, p. 252). In this poem, as in Swinburne's, the distinctions between Hermaphroditus's male and female attributes
are clearly defined. Yet, in the octave above there is no
anatomical sexual differentiation, and bisexuality is portrayed through a genderless physical image.

By focusing on the smile, Faulkner attempts to present
the emotional range of the original without Swinburne's
elaborate metaphorical embroidery. The enigmatic facial
expression functions as a visual referent through which the
inherent ambivalence of the subject's psychosexual position
can be explored. For example, whereas Swinburne presents
Hermaphroditus's basic dilemma through traditional romantic imagery ("Choose of two loves and cleave unto the best;
/ Two loves at either blossom of thy breast"),[21] Faulkner

retains his dominant metaphor, even though its use creates a rather awkward and convoluted grammatical structure (ll. 5–8). The syntactical density of this passage, together with the unswerving concentration on the decadent smile, suggests that Faulkner is striving for a structural and linguistic compression quite unlike the more discursive pattern of the original; it is as if the poetic task he set for himself here were to recast Swinburne's poem solely in terms of the imagery of its opening four lines.

Although the facial metaphor dominates Faulkner's poem, in Swinburne's it is only one of a number of figurative structures that work to maintain the precarious balance between his subject's beauty and abnormality. Throughout the poem, Swinburne's tone remains conjectural, and he refrains from directly evaluating the myth's psychological and moral implications. Faulkner, however, takes a much harsher view of Hermaphroditus's sexuality and, in the sestet, employs decidedly un-Swinburnian diction to emphasize its destructive unnaturalness:

> Weary thy mouth with smiling: canst thou bride
> Thyself with thee, or thine own kissing slake?
> Thy belly's waking doth itself deride
> With sleep's sharp absence, coming so awake;
> And near thy mouth thy twinned heart's grief doth hide
> For there's no breast between: it cannot break.   [*GB*, p. 61]

The language here is cruder ("belly," "deride," "break") and more vigorous ("canst thou bride / Thyself," "thine own kissing slake") than that of the octave, and, in its grammatical construction and general tone, seems closer to Elizabethan models than to Swinburne.[22] Thus, in transforming Swinburne's "Hermaphroditus," Faulkner grafts elements from two distinct literary sources, providing a new vision of the myth through the addition of expressive materials that derive from a more robust moral and aesthetic sensibility.[23]

Faulkner realizes the need for this kind of directness in
"Hermaphroditus," for in his version the protagonist is thrice
damned. Not only is he unable to attain sexual union (l. 9)
or sexual satisfaction (l. 10), he is, more importantly, unable
to experience profound emotion on any level; his androgy-
nous "twinned heart" remains whole in itself, physically
indivisible and therefore logically incapable of forming an
emotional union. This explicit criticism of the Hermaphroditus myth is radically different from the interpretation in
the model poem. Even though Swinburne's poem provides
the subject and, to a certain extent, the dominant pattern of
imagery, Faulkner's poem is informed by a literary sensibility that required a more critical assessment of Hermaphroditus and hence new combinations of expressive techniques.
In *Mosquitoes*, where sexual attitudes function as important
evaluative concepts, the "Hermaphroditus" sonnet becomes
a focal point for the discussion of sexual roles. In this context, Faulkner uses the poem as a loose metaphor for the
spiritual, social, and aesthetic decadence of the twenties.
One of the older, more positively portrayed characters comments on the poem, reinforcing Faulkner's interpretation of
the myth: "'"Hermaphroditus,"'" he read. 'That's what it's
about. It's a kind of dark perversion. Like a fire that don't
need any fuel, that lives on its own heat. . . . A kind of
sterile race: women too masculine to conceive, men too
feminine to beget. . . .'" (*M*, p. 252).[24]

The exercise of creatively reworking "Hermaphroditus"
in an attempt to analyze Swinburne's techniques firsthand
thus led Faulkner to discover solutions to aesthetic problems
of a personal kind, as Wright suggested. For Faulkner, conscious imitation could indeed become a process of self-
revelation, and in his apprentice period he reexamined a
surprisingly diverse group of existing poems, ranging from
Housman's ballad quatrains to Pound's experiments in free
verse.[25] Some of these exercises, such as the imitations of

Housman in Poems VII–XI of *A Green Bough*, proved to be dead ends, while others, like the Swinburne adaptations, provided structures and strategies that helped to advance his personal creative development.[26]

For example, the embarrassingly close—but clearly not parodic—imitations of Eliot's early verse that Faulkner collected in a handmade pamphlet entitled *Vision in Spring* gave him the opportunity to assimilate a whole battery of new techniques for dramatizing consciousness;[27] they may also have first alerted him to the possibility of dealing with the modulations of the mind itself as a viable literary subject.[28] Even on the evidence of the brief extracts quoted by Joseph Blotner, one can see Faulkner imitatively studying a good number of the overtly "modern" rhetorical devices developed by one who might reasonably be considered his "most advanced predecessor." Faulkner's "Love Song," for example, opens with a section that practically duplicates the middle section of Eliot's original:

> Shall I walk, then, through a corridor of profundities
> Carefully erect (I am taller than I look)
> To a certain door—and shall I dare
> To open it? I smooth my mental hair
> With an oft changed phrase that I revise again
> Until I have forgotten what it was at first;
> Settle my tie with: I have brought a book,
> Then seat myself with: We have passed the worst.[29]

This monologue, like Prufrock's, is replete with false starts, repetitions, and questions that require no answers. And if Faulkner blatantly ignores the ironic potential of Eliot's model, he effectively reproduces its artificially neutral diction, with its profusion of abstract and nondescriptive phrases ("corridor of profundities," "certain door," "mental hair"), which, along with the almost total absence of visual imagery, emphasizes the ordinary spoken word and contributes to the reader's feeling that he is confronted directly by unmediated groups of thoughts and mental images.

Less conspicuous, but even more significant, reliance on Eliot's models can be seen in "The Lilacs" (Poem I of *A Green Bough*,[30] one of Faulkner's more successful poems. Although the use of the lilac imagery and a formal social setting does suggest superficial features of Eliot's "Portrait of a Lady," Faulkner now extrapolates (as he had not done in the Prufrockian exercises) from the prototype's deeper structures and reexamines its underlying organizational principles rather than its more obvious linguistic or thematic elements. "The Lilacs" thus builds directly on the formal configuration of "Portrait of a Lady," in which fragmented images and distinct temporal units are juxtaposed by means of the minimally controlling frame of a dramatized consciousness.

As in "Portrait of a Lady," the tension in "The Lilacs" between the circumscribed past and ongoing present is expressed through a dialectic of voices. And Faulkner neatly separates the dramatis personae of the interior action—the flier and his dead comrades—from that of the external setting—the late afternoon tea party—by suspending the referent of the ambiguous "we three" of the opening paragraph until the poem's conclusion, where the reader learns that there is only one wounded aviator actually present and that the plural pronoun reflects the speaker's acute sense of his dead companions' presence.[31] Not only is the present scene, the hospital visiting day, with its social banalities, ironically juxtaposed to the more portentous and meaningful confrontations of past battles, but the past scenes themselves are also presented through a rhetoric of tension. Just as various temporal units in "Portrait of a Lady" are clearly identified and placed one against the other (the December afternoon of section 1 is aligned with the April sunset of section 2 and the October night of section 3), so in "The Lilacs" the evocations of the war are removed from the framing scene by explicit reference to the aerial battles' respective times and places: the convalescents' lawn party occurs on a late summer afternoon (par. 1), while the first flier describes a morning in May above the border of a wood (par. 3) and the second recalls a night raid over Mannheim "hung beneath the stars" (par. 7).

The specific imagery associated with each combat scene is similarly contrasted, both to the linen and lilacs of the party and to each other; hence the ascendant whiteness of the first flier's celebratory transcendence is juxtaposed to the second's descent into blackness. And although both scenes in the past implicitly comment on the initial speaker's mental, physical, and psychological predicament ("shot down / Last spring—Poor chap"), neither is rhetorically emphasized, and they remain separate visions, competing for attention, related to each other and to the framing sequence by virtue of the focal character's embracing consciousness. This is the locus or ground on which each scene reacts with the others, creating the tensions between past and present, life and death, combat and peace. The three-way dialectic, emphasized by argumentative conversational devices ("—Who?—shot down," "—Yes, you are right"), avoids a simple ethical dichotomy and allows alternative responses to war's destruction and its aftermath to assume equal rhetorical weight.

The importance of this poem in Faulkner's development is related to this complicated dialectical structure, a structure indebted to his study of Eliot and based on formal positioning and the creation of separate voices rather than on a more Swinburnian dependence on the strength of images alone. "The Lilacs" shows Faulkner working with distinct structural units, yet instead of organizing these parts into a whole by the use of causal connectives or chronological sequence, he creates a fragmented pattern that retains the individuality of each unit while exploiting its relationships to its structural contexts. This innovative and characteristically modern organizational strategy, with the devices employed to maintain it, stems from viewing literary form (as it seems Eliot does) as the fitting together of minimally related or totally disparate units of discourse, a montagelike structural principle that informs a good many of Faulkner's later works.

Although the choice of Swinburne and Eliot as "masters" surely offered the apprentice a considerable range of poetic methods and materials, Faulkner—perhaps striving consciously for Wright's "sedulous eclecticism"—did not confine his study to major figures. I have shown in detail elsewhere how, from 1919 to 1920, Faulkner not only explored symbolist conventions by "re-translating" Arthus Symons's version of Verlaine,[32] but also worked over sections of Robert Nichols's popular "A Faun's Holiday" in his own "L'Apres Midi d'un Faune," "Naiads' Song," and even in *The Marble Faun*, his first published book—borrowing extensively from the imagery, rhythms, and diction of its source. *The Marble Faun* is, in fact, Faulkner's most ambitious apprentice piece, and although it shows considerable organizational independence in its use of a fragmented formal pattern akin to that of "The Lilacs," its potential strength is ultimately undermined by a debilitating verbal dependence, an inability to shake off Nichols's fin de siècle stylizations.[33]

Although *The Marble Faun* is not as obviously a self-educational exercise as some of the other poems previously discussed, early readers who were already familiar with Nichols's prototype would undoubtedly have perceived the many correspondences between the two poems. This possibility apparently did not worry the young Faulkner, for here, as in the apprentice pieces in general, he leaves the workshop door open, exposing his literary schooling to public scrutiny. Whether his willingness so to exhibit his training procedures reflects his wholehearted commitment to Wright's belief in the absolute necessity of such a program for the development of creative talent, a neophyte's desire to see his work in print, or some combination of both, it must be remembered that while the Eliot studies were distributed privately and "Sapphics," "Naiads' Song," and the Verlaine translations were printed in a university newspaper, "L'Apres Midi d'un Faune" originally appeared in the *New Republic* and *The Marble Faun* was published as an original volume of verse.

To Phil Stone, the man most instrumental in furthering Faulkner's literary apprenticeship, the unmistakable derivativeness of his friend's first book seemed to require some kind of explanation. Faulkner, Stone declared in his preface to *The Marble Faun*, was a young man "of wide reading . . . deeply schooled in the poets and their technical trials and accomplishments." It was inevitable, he continued, "that this book should bear traces of other poets; probably all well-informed people have by this time learned that a poet does not spring full-fledged from the brow of Jove. He does have to be born with the native impulse, but he learns his trade from other poets by apprenticeship, just as a lawyer or a carpenter or a bricklayer learns his. It is inevitable that traces of apprenticeship should appear in a first book but a man who has real talent will grow, will leave these things behind, will finally bring forth a flower that could have grown in no garden but his own. All that is needed—granted the original talent—is work and unflinching honesty" (*MF*, pp. 7–8). Stone's emphasis on "schooling," "apprenticeship," and "honesty" ("honesty" appears in the preface three times) indicates a nervous awareness of the quantity and extent of Faulkner's use of literary models, coupled with a concern that readers perceiving such "traces of apprenticeship" might possibly misconstrue the author's motives.

Stone, like Wright, stressed the importance of learning "the trade" by imitative apprenticeship as a necessary first step to self-revelation and creative originality. Given Faulkner's lack of formal education, his commitment to learning "all he could" about the craft of writing, and his overriding sense of literary ambition, it is easy to see why he should take that step so firmly and decisively, and why, more particularly, he should begin with verse—poetry being traditionally valued above prose forms. That Faulkner's period of poetic composition was limited almost entirely to the initial stages of his career, and that he would eventually make his name in another literary medium, may be attributed as much to the painstaking and to some extent repetitive deliberateness of the educational process undergone, as to the incompatibility between the requirements of verse and his individual rhetorical powers.[34] In 1957 Faulkner recalled: "I wrote poetry when I was a young man till I found that I—that it was bad poetry, would never be first-rate poetry" (*FU*, p. 21). But although his initial commitment to poetry proved to be something of a dead end in itself, it marked a crucial stage in his literary apprenticeship, which was always to be a process of learning from negative as well as from positive experiences.

Critics have been quick to point out those aspects of Faulkner's verse—the tired conventions and debilitating diction—which he had to leave behind. But their stress on his dependence on "the pallid poetic code of the late Victorians" has caused them to ignore those features of the verse on which he would build—such as the organizational patterns of "The Lilacs" and *The Marble Faun*—as well as the larger educational procedures through which they were discovered.[35] If Faulkner in later years referred to himself, with some justification, as a failed poet, he could also, and with no less justification, have insisted that it was only through trying and failing in poetry that he eventually found his way to his extraordinary success in prose fiction. He might, in any case, have concurred in Wright's judgment that the "ability to write great poetry is an excellent preparation for the writing of great prose."[36]

2.
The Curse of Tongues
Apprenticeship in Prose

Wright had argued that the writing of poetry should be an ideal exercise for the writing of prose; Faulkner himself spoke of his turning to fiction as the action of a "failed poet." But there is little enough of Faulkner the poet in "Landing in Luck" (1919), his first published work of prose fiction (*EP*, pp. 42–50). It exhibits practically none of the linguistic and metaphorical exuberance that marks his poetic exercises at this time, and its expressive range fails to equal even that of his contemporaneous reviews. The stock plot, moreover, bears a closer resemblance to commercial magazine fiction than to literary art forms,[1] and, at first glance, it would appear that Faulkner initially approached narrative expression with creative presuppositions distinctly different from, and less consciously artistic than, those which guided his other literary productions of this period. The uncharacteristic nature of this story, with its flat style and unusual expressive restraint, however, is most probably due less to Faulkner's personal aesthetic attitudes than to the particular publishing policy of *The Mississippian*, the University of Mississippi's newspaper. "Landing in Luck" first appeared in a column headed "Weekly Short Story Edited by Professor Erwin" (*EP*, p. 125), and Professor Erwin's blue pencil might very well be largely responsible for what now seems its totally atypical mode.

A much more representative and revealing example of Faulkner's apprentice prose is "The Hill" (*EP*, pp. 90–92), a brief sketch published under its own title in *The Mississippian* about two-and-a-half years after "Landing in Luck." Like *The Marble Faun*, though on a considerably smaller scale, this prose poem explores imaginative transcendence through a structure of antithetical images and concludes with a similar, albeit less effective, evocation of vision denied.[2] This theme remained important to Faulkner, especially during the early stages of his career, and a few years later, probably in the beginning of 1925, he wrote "Nympholepsy," a recently discovered story that can be seen as a more expansive, and more realistic, reworking of essentially the same materials.[3] While the curiously titled "Nympholepsy" is perhaps the more polished piece,[4] "The Hill" is more interesting as a document in the history of Faulkner's literary development, for its minimal narrative line and almost negligible characterization pose few formal or technical restrictions and make it the perfect vehicle for linguistic and syntactical experimentation. Indeed, it remains probably the best, and certainly the most significant, example of Faulkner's creative prose until the publication of the sketches that appeared in the New Orleans literary magazine *The Double Dealer* in 1925.

The prose of "The Hill" is marked by uninhibited metaphorical elaboration, impressionistic description, and an obvious concern for the musical and rhythmic aspects of language; it also exhibits (as his poetry had often done) a concomitant disregard for syntactical structure, grammatical norms, and even, in some instances, semantic content. Faulkner thus subordinates coherent meaning to lyrical expression and gives his poetic instincts free rein, expanding characteristic image patterns and modifying rhetorical strategies to fit the requirements of the prose poem's more discursive form—even, in some instances, directly importing materials and techniques from his own verse. "The Hill" focuses on an unusual and unexpected moment of visionary release that violently interrupts a farm laborer's homeward journey. From its opening lines Faulkner makes it quite clear that the controlling event, the unnamed worker's ascent, is as much an imaginative endeavor as a physical climb, and he thus immediately establishes a structure that involves the interaction of figurative and literal expressive devices. It is therefore not surprising that by the end of the first paragraph, the naturalistically described protagonist, with "loose jacket and trousers" and "thick uncombed hair above his stubby quiet face," has become poetically stylized, transformed into a "shadow" engaged in "futile puppet-like activity . . . while time and life terrifically passed him and left him behind" (*EP*, p. 90).

The shadow image, moreover, metaphorically charts the progress of his imaginative transcendence; thus, while his "monstrous shadow lay like a portent upon the church," he senses the immanence of revelation: "and for a moment he had almost grasped something alien to him" (*EP*, p. 91). Similarly, when he first contemplates the aesthetically patterned panorama of the motionless "valley stretched beneath him," he observes how "his shadow . . . lay across it, quiet and enormous" (*EP*, p. 91). The use of the "shadow" as a ghostly image of ego-extension, as a figurative "double," taken together with the twilight setting and the evocation of mechanical motion (in the opening paragraph), forms an important imaginative complex that underlies much of Faulkner's early work. This complex contributes, for example, to his frequent characterizations of commedia dell'arte figures, especially in his early play *The Marionettes*, where the "shade of Pierrot" acts while his corporeal self sleeps, and prefigures, moreover, the creation of that other shadow-obsessed dreamer, Quentin Compson, who is himself caught up in twilight, "that quality of light, as if time really had stopped for a while" (*SF*, pp. 209–10).[5]

At the conclusion of "The Hill," after "the sun released him" and it becomes clear that the protagonist's transcendence is truly denied, Faulkner replaces the shadow imagery with an elaborate, but almost entirely unrelated, evocation of nightfall: "Here, in the dusk, nymphs and fauns might riot to a shrilling of thin pipes, to a shivering and hissing of cymbals in a sharp volcanic abasement beneath a tall icy star" (*EP*, p. 92). This strenuously poetic description, if indeed comprehensible in itself (what does "volcanic abasement" mean?), bears almost no thematic or formal relation to even the most lyrical passages in the remainder of "The Hill" and is imported with little rhetorical or linguistic modification from some more congenial pastoral context, such as a draft of *The Marble Faun* or, perhaps, even "Twilight"—a verse equivalent of an analogous vision presented through similar images.[6] Although not especially effective in this case, the purely linguistic resolution of "The Hill" does, however, point toward Faulkner's later habit of finding "poetic" conclusions for otherwise unresolved narratives, and it thus may even faintly anticipate the essentially verbal closures of *Soldiers' Pay*, *Flags in the Dust*, and *The Sound and the Fury*.

In other sections of "The Hill," however, Faulkner effectively adapts poetic devices and integrates them into the sketch's larger rhetorical structure. In the third paragraph, for example, in order to contrast directly the panoramic and proximate views of the hamlet and thereby formally oppose images of aesthetic stasis and quotidian activity, he employs the techniques of extended grammatical negation with which he had first experimented three years earlier in his adaptation of Swinburne's "Sapphics." Swinburne had used nega-

tive constructions to illustrate Sappho's emotional detachment
through an evocation of her indifference to Aphrodite's grief:

> she saw not
> Tears for laughter darken immortal eyelids,
> Heard not about her
>
> Fearful fitful wings of the doves departing,
> Saw not how the bosom of Aphrodite
> Shook with weeping, saw not her shaken raiment,
> Saw not her hands wrung;[7]

Faulkner, on the other hand, describes the same scene from
the goddess's perspective and, unlike Swinburne, stresses
Aphrodite's profound loss through a presentation of aural
and visual images that remain unperceived:

> She looks not back, she looks not back to where
> The nine crowned muses about Apollo
> Stand like nine Corinthian columns singing
> In clear evening.
>
> She sees not the Lesbians kissing mouth
> To mouth across lute strings, drunken with singing,
> Nor the white feet of the Oceanides
> Shining and unsandalled.   [*EP*, p. 51]

This technique allows Faulkner a double focus, since it
keeps grammatical emphasis on the sentence's subject and
its negated object, thus calling attention to Aphrodite's grief
without diminishing the concomitant depiction of its un-
observed cause. It is, therefore, extremely effective for economically juxtaposing antithetical perspectives or for
revealing the ironic disparity between a limited point of
view and an unrestricted, omniscient vision. So in "The
Hill," Faulkner first presents the vista from the hillcrest—
"a motionless mosaic of tree and house" (*EP*, p. 91)—and
then zooms in to evoke moving objects and changing con-

ditions of which the laborer is intimately aware, but which exist totally outside his present perceptual field. A whole paragraph is devoted to a description of this unseen scene. As in "Sapphics," loss and absence are rhetorically foregrounded; the emphasis falls on those things that remain unperceived and on emotions that remain unfelt. Thus, without disturbing the arrested, immanently transcendent moment, Faulkner offers an image of the reality invisibly underlying the distant imaginative design so that "the hamlet which was home to him" (*EP*, p. 92) becomes structurally aligned with the alternative, timeless vision of aesthetic repose.[8]

Given the elaborate metaphorical structure, range of language, direct appropriation of poetic strategies, and general aesthetic orientation of "The Hill," it seems Faulkner was attempting from an early date to create a prose style that would achieve something of the linguistic density of poetry. But the evidence of "Landing in Luck" would suggest that "The Hill" was an exercise in a particular style rather than an indication of a total commitment to that style. In *The Creative Will* Wright had been critical of the development of personal literary styles. According to Wright, "the writer strives to develop a certain technical manner, and he uses it, without variation, throughout his work. This technical manner is called his 'style,' whereas it is only a rigid and dogmatic repudiation of style. What is commonly termed 'style' in literature is little more than an idiosyncrasy of expression—a mannerism."[9] In his first review of fiction, Faulkner shows his awareness of the creative limits imposed by the adoption of too personal a linguistic manner: Joseph Hergesheimer's "ability to write flawless prose" (*EP*, p. 103) is censured on the ground that it was achieved by directing his imaginative energies solely toward the pursuit of style. He sees Hergesheimer, consequently, as "enslaved by words" to an extent only exceeded by Poe (*EP*, p. 101),

referring to him in another early review as a "decayed Pater."[10]

Wright had also invoked Walter Pater to indicate the det-
rimental effects of stylistic homogeneity: "True style—one
which attests to mastery—is an ability to change one's manner at random so as to harmonise the expression with the
thing expressed. A great stylist can write suavely, simply
and delicately, as well as robustly, complexly and brutally.
Shakespeare is a stylist. Pater is the negation of style."[11] As
late as 1941 Faulkner apparently recalled precisely this for-
mulation when he told one of his first critics, Warren Beck:
"I had rather read Shakespeare, bad puns, bad history, taste
and all, than Pater, and that I had a damn sight rather fail at
trying to write Shakespeare than to write all of Pater over
again so he couldn't have told it himself if you fired it point
blank at him through an amplifier" (*L*, p. 142).

Although Faulkner would later develop a highly recog-
nizable style, he can be seen in his first prose works—in
"The Hill" and particularly in those sketches and stories that
appeared in *The Double Dealer* and the New Orleans *Times-
Picayune* during 1925—as striving to achieve expressive
diversity, "the ability to change the manner of presentation
at will," rather than a readily identifiable personal voice.
The stylistically and formally heterogenous New Orleans
prose pieces are less notable for their intrinsic literary merit
than for their remarkable rhetorical variety and technical
virtuosity. They are, it is true, decidedly less derivative than
the early poetry and include no obvious examples of texts
designed chiefly as reexaminations of existing formal models; even so, much of the work produced during this period
reflects a similar concern for aesthetic apprenticeship and a
conscious attempt to achieve "perfect mobility and plasticity."[12]

The deliberateness of this educational process is nowhere
more apparent than in the eleven stylistically distinct prose

poems that comprise "New Orleans." This text, which appeared in the January/February issue of *The Double Dealer* (*NO*, pp. 3–14), the literary magazine that had previously published one of Faulkner's poems, attempts to evoke the racial, social, and ethnic variety of New Orleans by selectively focusing on representative members of the city's population. Criticism of the sketch has concentrated on the individual figures presented and Faulkner's means of characterizing them, but the brief monologues seem, in fact, to be less concerned with character delineation than with the exercise of linguistic skills.[13] It becomes quickly apparent that "New Orleans" as a whole subordinates formal and thematic coherence to a display of sheer verbal dexterity. The speakers function primarily as disembodied voices, providing vocal or thematic centers for the various expressive modes. In terms of any larger organizing pattern, the individual sections remain fundamentally separate units, related to each other only through verbal repetitions (such phrases as "lump of moist dirt," "I am old," and "Ah God" appear in several of the monologues) and ironies dependent on formal juxtapositions: "The Priest," for instance, is flanked by "Wealthy Jew" and "Frankie and Johnny," "The Artist" by "The Beggar" and "Magdalen."

The conspicuous absence of significant action or psychological detail reveals the degree to which Faulkner conceived of the monologues essentially as vehicles for linguistic exploration, and they do demonstrate, whatever their weaknesses, a prodigious range of prose styles and rhetorical strategies. The series begins with what might be termed the allusive-prophetic mode of "Wealthy Jew" (*NO*, pp. 3–4), which revolves around a quotation from Théophile Gautier's *Mademoiselle de Maupin* ("I love three things: gold; marble and purple; splendor, solidity, color"), employs an oratorical voice ("O ye mixed races, with your blood mingled and thinned and lost"), takes a historical perspective (including references to "Ahenobarbus' gardens," Alexander, Caesar, Napoleon, and Passchendaele), and contains Conradian echoes.[14] Next comes the allusive-decadent style of "The Priest" (*NO*, pp. 4 5), whose subject matter might very well have been inspired by Sherwood Anderson's mono- logue "Testament (containing songs of one who would be a priest)" in the immediately preceding number of *The Double Dealer*.[15] The tone of "The Priest," however, is character- ized by its quotation from Swinburne's erotic lament "In the Orchard" ("hold my hair fast, and kiss me through it—so: Ah, God, ah God, that day should be so soon!")[16] and its juxtaposition of late-romantic similes ("How like birds with golden wings the measured bell notes fly") with sonorous litanies, possibly echoing the early Joyce ("Ave, Maria; deam gratiam"). Further along one finds the stylized street diction of "Frankie and Johnny" (*NO*, pp. 5–6), with its experientially derived similes ("When I seen you coming down the street back yonder it was like them two ferry boats hadn't seen each other until then, and they would stop when they met"), and the impressionistic "Magdalen" (*NO*, pp. 12–13), which concludes with a phrase from Robert Nich- ols's "Fulfilment."[17] The expressionistic "The Longshore- man" (*NO*, p. 9) is built around strings of rhythmic metaphors ("Streaks of sunlight cutting the wall's shadow, slide up me, barring my overalls and my black hands with stripes of gold"), and the discursive-colloquial mode of "The Cop" (*NO*, pp. 10–11) offers such stolid banalities as "Anyway, I prefer to believe that this creature fronting the world bravely in a blue coat and a silver shield is quite a fellow, after all." Finally comes the comprehensively metaphorical strategy of "The Tourist" (*NO*, pp. 13–14), whose extended person- ification of New Orleans as a "courtesan" living "in an at- mosphere of a bygone and more gracious age" recalls Lafcadio Hearn's popular "The Glamour of New Orleans," reprinted in *The Double Dealer* three years earlier.[18]

Although extremely broad in scope, this stylistic tour de force is limited to purely linguistic exploration and represents only one example of Faulkner's concrete examination of prose forms.[19] Wright had repeatedly emphasized that only "when all the potential qualities which are at the disposal of the creators of great literature shall have been recognised and mastered, will the writer's medium be sufficiently plastic and complete to permit of full freedom of expression." He stated, moreover, that an aesthetic "sensitivity is of no value unless one possesses the capacity to transmit it through some medium; and, other things being equal, the artist with the greatest technical facility will be able to set down his vision with the purest intensity."[20] Although Faulkner would later disagree with this final dictum, stressing the importance of initial inspiration, thematic strength, and creative compulsion over formal dexterity, a belief in technical experimentation directed toward a broadening of expressive facility remained an integral part of his personal aesthetic. In a 1955 interview he stated that in order to acquire the necessary creative tools, an aspiring writer must "have the desire to learn, the patience to learn and an infinite capacity to experiment" (*LG*, p. 182). "New Orleans" provides direct and early evidence of Faulkner's own "capacity to experiment," his willingness to examine and assimilate the basic conventions of his newly adopted literary medium. Perhaps through this exercise he discovered his almost protean technical range—as well as his remarkable capacity for stylistic ventriloquism—and realized, as he said of himself in an autobiographical poem entitled "Bill," that "with the gift of tongues he was accursed."[21]

During his 1925 residence in New Orleans, Faulkner continued to develop his "gift" through an ever-widening exploration of stylistic modes and rhetorical strategies, including a number of works that are closely related to "New Orleans" and that show him, for the first time since "Landing in

Luck," working directly with techniques of sequential action and problems of narrative form. It is impossible, on the evidence at present available, to determine accurately whether the more protracted versions of "The Cobbler" (*NO*, pp. 66–69), published in May 1925 in the *Times-Picayune*, or of "The Priest" (which remained unpublished during Faulkner's lifetime)[22] preceded the compositions of the identically entitled monologues in *The Double Dealer*—making the shorter pieces, in effect, formal abridgements—or whether, paralleling the apparent textual relationship between "Nympholepsy" and "The Hill," they constitute later revisions and structural extensions of the "New Orleans" material.[23] But, regardless of the order of composition, the respective versions of the two sketches are distinguished by more than differences in style, and the substantive alterations between texts involve additions to (or subtractions from) the informing patterns of action.

The two longer versions of the sketches (like "Nympholepsy," incidentally) are organized around rudimentary plot structures significantly more developed than the implicit lines of action that are present in the shorter pieces. One might say therefore that in the extended versions each sketch's central conflict has been given a specific narrative shape— as in the *Times-Picayune* text of "The Cobbler" where, through a brief flashback, a sequence of actions gives substance to the speaker's profound sense of loss; in the shorter piece the reason for his wife's absence is never provided. Similarly, in the typescript version of "The Priest," the primary opposition between spirituality and sensuality, which had been expressed through a purely verbal antithesis, now becomes manifest in mimetic action: for the priest, "girls going home from work . . . became symbols of grace and beauty, of impulses antedating Christianity," and "men through with work for the day" are perceived solely in terms of their imminent contact with women—"going home to comfortable dinners, to wives and children; or to bachelor rooms to prepare for engagements with mistresses or sweethearts—always women."[24]

In the same way, the longer story's first two sentences establish a setting and narrative context that has no parallel in *The Double Dealer* piece: "His novitiate was almost completed. Tomorrow he would be confirmed, tomorrow he would achieve that complete mystical union with the Lord, which he had so passionately desired."[25] The sketch thus opens at a climacteric moment in the priest's life and immediately introduces the fundamental disparity between novitiate and priesthood in terms of a common yet symbolically suggestive point of transition—today's relative freedom versus tomorrow's ordination. The basic tension and imagery of the longer story is directly built on this temporal division; in the "New Orleans" version, on the other hand, the central antithesis between night and day ("Evening like a nun" / "Ah God, ah God, that day should be so soon") has nothing specific behind it—no concrete referent—and the conflict it evokes remains abstract and poetic.

In these pieces the same subject matter is thus given significantly different treatment: the "New Orleans" texts are informed by predominantly atemporal and poetic principles; the more substantial versions are organized by sequential actions and constitute true narratives. If these pairs of texts represent some kind of deliberate literary experiment, they attest to more than a stylistic versatility, for they show Faulkner effectively presenting identical material using very different linguistic and rhetorical strategies.

The scope and further direction of this prose exploration is indicated by the sketches, published and unpublished, that occupied Faulkner during the remainder of his 1925 New Orleans residence. In these stories, Faulkner not only experimented with various ways of organizing actions—including conventional plots, episodic designs, framed tales, and other more innovative structures—but also with various narrative perspectives, such as dramatized first person, omniscient third person, free indirect speech (*erlebte Rede*)— where, to put it simply, "the narrator takes on the speech of the character"[26]—and so forth. Taken together, in fact, these stories can be seen as a kind of deliberate course in fictional discourse, a set of creative exercises based on the aesthetic permutations derived from the combinations of such diverse structural and linguistic forms. Faulkner grouped some of these pieces under the title "Sinbad in New Orleans," and it is perhaps not too fanciful to see the writer himself as the explorer figure actively charting the imaginative territory of his newly adopted medium.

A number of these apprentice sketches ("Jealousy," "Chance," and "The Rosary," for example) involve a rhetorically unassertive third-person narrator and conventional plot structures.[27] And though, in terms of Faulkner's prose experimentation, they are probably the least interesting of all the New Orleans sketches, these *Times-Picayune* stories, like the earlier "Landing in Luck," do show that he was also trying his hand at basic techniques of commercial magazine fiction—techniques, so he would sometimes later imply, that he never properly assimilated.[28] Like innumerable popular tales and traditional short stories, they are patterned on simple ironic peripeteia—O. Henryesque reversals—and their narrative force and formal coherence thus reside primarily in the thematic and structural relevance of their climaxes.[29] Faulkner's dénouements, however, though properly coincident with the moment of dramatic reversal, bear little relationship to developing characterizations and, unlike effective plot closures, invariably hinge on what are perceived as wholly arbitrary events—such as the automobile accident in "Chance," Mr. Harris's unknown demise in "The Rosary," or the explosion of the antique pistol in "Jealousy." There are, however, examples of more successful experiments with conventional plots in the *Times-Picayune* fiction, including "The Kingdom of God" (*NO*, pp. 55–60), where the central narrative tensions are informed by character relationships extending beyond the climactic change in fortune, and "Country Mice" (*NO*, pp. 108–20) or "The Liar" (*NO*, pp. 92–103), where Faulkner effectively adds flesh to the skeletal sequences of events by providing a dramatized narrator who, during the process of recitation, becomes intimately involved with the patterns of action and thus is personally affected by their reversals.

The majority of the *Times-Picayune* sketches, however, are unified around revelatory episodes rather than traditional plots and are directed more toward character delineation than toward the development of sequential action or the creation of narrative suspense. Some of these texts, such as "Mirrors of Chartres Street" (*NO*, pp. 15–18) or "Damon and Pythias Unlimited" (*NO*, pp. 19–27), employ a dramatized first-person narrator who remains intellectually and emotionally detached from the stories' humble events, abstractly pondering "the mutability of mankind" or "how imaginative atrophy seems to follow . . . automatic food and bathtubs per capita" (*NO*, p. 19), while providing analytical descriptions of the urban street life that surrounds him. Other examples of episodic sketches involve a more sympathetic first-person narrator who bears a certain autobiographical resemblance to the young Faulkner and who, like his artist companion William Spratling, attempts to "capture" the subjects who appear before him. In "Episode" (*NO*, pp. 104–7), for example, the physical posture assumed by an old woman posing for Spratling becomes emblematic for the narrator, first of her entire past life and then, echoing Pater's appreciation of *La Gioconda*, of women in general: "Ah, women, who have but one eternal age! And that is no age" (*NO*, p. 107).

Other models for Faulkner and Spratling include the Christ-

like David of "Out of Nazareth" (*NO*, pp. 46–54). David is
portrayed partly through his own primitive first-person narrative, which is incorporated into the text, according to the
narrator, "word for word, as he wrote it," even though "some
of the words mean nothing, as far as I know (and words are
my meat and bread and drink), but to change them would
be to destroy David himself" (*NO*, p. 53). Similarly, in
"Peter," a sketch that remained unpublished during Faulkner's lifetime, a black prostitute's mulatto child—"an inci-
dental coin minted between the severed yet similar despairs
of two races"—provides further subject matter for artistic
and literary scrutiny. While Spratling draws the boy in "a
shabby littered court," lusty language from the adjacent brothel
(presented as in a playscript) becomes interspersed with
Peter's innocent ramblings, and the text concludes with an
extended poetical lament tracing the narrator's thoughts as
he watches "the noon become afternoon . . . in spite of art
and vice and everything else which makes a world; hearing
the broken phrases of a race answering quickly to the com-
pulsions of the flesh and then going away, temporarily freed
from the body, to sweat and labor and sing; doomed again
to repair to a temporary satisfaction; fleeting, that cannot
last. The world: death and despair, hunger and sleep. Hunger that tolls the body along until life becomes tired of the
burden."[30] This lyrical termination, like the ending of "The
Hill," operates primarily through "poetic" means. Although
somewhat repetitious, it provides a kind of thematic um-
brella for the text's juxtaposed voices and closes the narrative through a rhetoric of rhythmic abstractions, which, by
their progressively greater generalization, place Peter's life
and racial heredity within a larger, and less critical, ethical
framework.

In other evocations of the ethnic or racial diversity of
New Orleans life, such as "Home" (*NO*, pp. 28–33), "The
Cobbler" (*NO*, pp. 66–69), or "Sunset" (*NO*, pp. 76–85),

Faulkner leaves behind the detached, dramatized first-person narrator (or narrative team) and focuses directly on the central character. In "Home," for instance, extended *erlebte Rede* presentations gradually develop into what may be termed a technique of interior catechism (complete with dramatized questions and answers) that effectively charts the progress of Jean-Baptiste's mental vacillations as the ethical ramifications of his desperate decision to become a criminal impinge on his consciousness. Other experiments with nondramatized narrators include the recently published "Frankie and Johnny," an extended version of the "Frankie and Johnny" section of "New Orleans" dating from about the same time, which presents the couple's subsequent relationship and its complications.[31] The narrator provides social and hereditary details of Frankie's background, as well as descriptions of Johnny's occupation and aspirations. Yet, despite the naturalistic framework and causally related pattern of events, there is no resolution of the plot and, as in "Peter" and "The Hill," Faulkner terminates the narrative (as he would do so often in the future) with a fundamentally poetic structure. Frankie thus ponders her pregnancy through an elaborate series of seasonal metaphors that ascend to a verbal apotheosis: "She felt as impersonal as the earth itself: she was a strip of fecund seeded ground lying under the moon and wind and stars of the four seasons, lying beneath grey and sunny weather since before time was measured; and that now was sleeping away a dark winter waiting for her own spring with all the pain and passion of its inescapable ends to a beauty which shall not pass from the earth."[32] This description provides the force of closure through its syntactical pattern (the movement of the phrases toward stasis), its implicit universality ("since before time was measured"), and its explicit terminal allusions ("inescapable ends," "shall not pass from the earth"). The fact that the entire description closely associates Frankie with nature also adds to its closural properties: as Victor Shklovsky has pointed out, allusions to natural processes at the very end of a text present so general a thematic image that we have no difficulty in satisfactorily connecting it to antecedent narrative materials.[33]

Faulkner employs a different, although similarly verbal, narrative resolution in "The Kid Learns" (*NO*, pp. 86–91), which is also related to the Frankie and Johnny material. Here, however, the closure involves a radical shift to the symbolic rather than a flight into the poetic. The appearance of "little sister Death" (probably derived from St. Francis's "Canticle of Creatures") not only distinctly foreshadows Quentin's female companion in *The Sound and the Fury*, but also shows Faulkner for the first time placing an allegorical figure in a predominantly realistic context—thus ending the text with a leap from the mimetic to the explicitly emblematic.[34]

"Sunset" provides an even more innovative and extended example of Faulkner's exploration of mixed modes, in that it incorporates two distinct and antithetical forms of narrative report and is designed principally to exploit, at every level, the thematically parallel (but stylistically and rhetorically disparate) explanations of a single sequence of actions: the brief and objective newspaper story, flatly describing "A Black Desperado Slain," versus the more elaborate, inward-focused, and sympathetic chronicle of the protagonist's tragic misadventures (*NO*, pp. 76–85).[35] A similar, though severely truncated, instance of this rhetorical strategy informs an unpublished typescript fragment that, in subject matter and general tone, appears closely related to the Al Jackson letters—the humorous correspondence between Sherwood Anderson and Faulkner about the exploits of the mythical Jackson family, which partly appeared in *Mosquitoes*.[36] This brief, untitled typescript provides, like "Sunset," two textually distinct narrative lines: in this case, a first-person travelogue or memoir (tracing, among other things, the founding of Mandeville, Louisiana, and the development of an aquatic sheep business) and a series of annotations, including further biographical evidence, ostensibly written by someone performing an editorial function. The pseudo-scholarly stance of the editor provides additional ironic commentary on what is already fairly ludicrous material: "On the return voyage my mother, reaching for a nightcap before retiring, fell through a port hole. It is from this pre-natal influence that I get my penchant for wearing a nightcap with evening clothes." The footnote to this passage reads: "His other maritime habits, such as wearing overshoes in bathing and wearing a yachting cap on the street, come from [a] disease acquired while frog-ranching, and his later successful assosiation [sic] with the fish industry."[37] Like the Al Jackson letters themselves, this fragment shows Faulkner experimenting with the tall-tale genre and perhaps attempting to assimilate some of the conventions of exaggerated oral humor.

When compared to the prodigious expressive range of Faulkner's career, that of the New Orleans prose might not appear so exceptional or significant. At the time, however, Faulkner's technical facility seemed so impressive that Anderson—from whatever mixed motives of critical principle, personal friendship, or simple envy—warned him that it might become an end in itself: "You've got too much talent. You can do it too easy, in too many different ways. If you're not careful, you'll never write anything."[38] Although this expressive virtuosity may have worried Anderson, it seems to have been exactly what Faulkner, at this stage of his career, was striving for. Moving from the restrictive idiom of his verse, aware of Wright's suggestion for the development of a "plastic" prose style, Faulkner was energetically searching not for his voice but for his voices. Those voices, which he discovered in and through these exercises, significantly contributed to the stylistic variation that would make *Soldiers' Pay* so distinctive a first novel and the full body of his fiction so remarkable for its persistently renewed diversity.

3.
Learning a Little about Writing
Faulkner's First Novel

By the summer of 1925, Faulkner was totally committed to a literary vocation, and while working on the heterogeneous *Times-Picayune* fiction and an impressive number of concurrent projects—including some verse,[1] the Al Jackson letters, and at least two articles (one of which won $10 for discussing "What Is Wrong with Marriage" in 250 words or less)[2]—he completed the typescript of what was to become *Soldiers' Pay*, his first novel.[3] Although there appear to be no sections of *Soldiers' Pay* designed exclusively as linguistic or formal exercises, the novel as a whole exhibits a considerable range of experimentation, particularly with respect to deliberate variations in language and narrative strategy. Its overall style, in fact, can be viewed as the result, or more properly the extension, of the contemporaneous prose explorations examined in the preceding chapter. Consequently, it is in *Soldiers' Pay*, much more than in the sketches, that Faulkner demonstrates the extent to which his inherent "curse of tongues" could be developed into the kind of truly expressive medium advocated by Wright. Perhaps even more importantly, this first extended work in prose fiction gave Faulkner "room" enough to broaden, intensify, and further individualize those fragmented organizational strategies that had informed the most significant of his previous work.

The unusual diversity of language, together with the apparent disconnectedness of its formal design, makes *Soldiers' Pay*, on first glance, seem a very self-conscious, mannered, and somewhat static novel, and it is not surprising that critics, looking back from the vantage point of Faulkner's later achievements, should have found it an odd starting point for his fictional career. But, viewed as a stage in an ongoing apprenticeship devoted to the deliberate development of linguistic flexibility, appropriation of the full range of available fictional techniques, and refinement of purely personal approaches to literary form, *Soldiers' Pay* can not only be neatly fitted into the larger pattern of Faulkner's aesthetic growth, but can also be shown to be the most significant precursor of *The Sound and the Fury*, the text that was to transform and transcend all previous experimentation, boldly marking Faulkner's transition from apprentice to master.

The radical stylistic virtuosity of *Soldiers' Pay* is nowhere more apparent than in its striking and even disconcerting first section, which details the returning soldiers' initial confrontation with the postwar world. Although Faulkner worked with diverse rhetorical and linguistic structures in the *Times-Picayune* fiction, there is nothing in the sketches, or indeed in any of the apprentice work, that would prepare one for the distinctive amalgam of slang, quotation, bombast, and sheer nonsense that he created in the initial scenes of *Soldiers' Pay* in an attempt to express the ramifications of the veterans' homecoming. It is especially significant that he prefaced this section with the dialogue between Achilles and Mercury—the entirely fictitious excerpt from a nonexistent

"Old Play"—for not only does this example of typical barracks humor point toward the military subject matter, comic
tone, and essentially dramatic method of the novel's introductory episode, it also, and more importantly, alerts the
reader to the section's deliberately allusive and heavily stylized mode of discourse.

In the epigraph, as in the remainder of the first section,
the authentic language of the war—the explicit references
to military protocol, battles, regimental tags, and contemporary jingoism—no longer has relevant contexts or specific referents and thus becomes literally and chronologically
the language of an "Old Play." Faulkner heightens this linguistic anachronism in order to portray the profound displacement of the soldiers and, as the chapter develops, merges
the now outmoded language of the war with other more
exaggerated and conventionally artificial linguistic media,
thus creating an elaborate verbal hybrid, replete with snatches
of bawdy songs, political rhetoric, music hall routines, and
fragmented literary quotations. In this way, references to the
"Battle of Coonyak" and its ridiculously changeable death
toll ("Ten men killed. Maybe fifteen. Maybe hundred.")
become first melodramatically elevated ("Poor children at
home saying 'Alice, where art thou?'") and then are batheti-
cally undercut ("Yeh, Alice. Where in hell are you? That
other bottle. What'n'ell have you done with it?" [*SP*, p. 9]).
Similarly, the typical battlefield order, "Fall in when fire call
blows, boys" (*SP*, p. 19), becomes an invitation to drinking;
the train conductor's uniform comes to represent, in succession, that of an "Admiral," "Colonel," "Sergeant," and
"Captain"; and the discovery of "Hank White," an insen-
tiently drunk soldier from "the middle-weight mule-wiper's
battalion," becomes the subject for a farcical deathbed ora-
tion, which includes an ironic description of an appropriate
military memorial: "Hank! Don't you recognize this weeping voice, this soft hand on your brow? General . . . will

you be kind enough to take charge of the remains? I will deputize these kind strangers to stop at the first harness factory we pass and have a collar suitable for mules made of dogwood with the initials H. W. in forget-me-nots" (*SP*, p. 19).

The first paragraph of *Soldiers' Pay*, however, is devoid of this cynical and exuberant style, opening instead with a detached summary description of Julian Lowe, a flying cadet who, because of his nickname, "One Wing," and his hopeless naiveté, bears a certain resemblance to Cadet Thompson of "Landing in Luck." Because "they stopped the war on him" before he had a chance to prove his valor, just as "they" had done to Cadet Faulkner, he may also have some autobiographical significance.[4] In any case, from the outset Lowe is portrayed wholly in terms of his abortive military experience, and his frankly romantic response to the war, entirely distinct from that of the other soldiers in the novel, stems directly from his prematurely truncated career—the cause of his pervasive and "disgusted sorrow."

This very brief, almost naturalistic portrait, however, is profoundly undercut by the arrival of Yaphank, a drunken veteran with a properly "tortured hat," whose grotesquely military self-introduction immediately parodies Lowe's and inaugurates the distinctively stylized language that controls the episode: "I got your number. Number no thousand no hundred and naughty naught Private (very private) Joe Gilligan, late for parade, late for fatigue, late for breakfast when breakfast is late. The statue of liberty ain't never seen me, and if she do, she'll have to 'bout face" (*SP*, p. 8). On meeting another, even more intoxicated, veteran—Yaphank's "travelling companion"—Lowe can think only of "devastated France" and associate the unnamed soldier with his own vicarious experience of the war ("swimming his memory through the adenoidal reminiscences of Captain Bleyth, an R.A.F. pilot") while Yaphank confronts the drunken and immobile soldier with a barrage of allusive insult. Sheer verbalization concerns Yaphank more than his sodden friend's military career: "Move over, you ancient mariner. Move over, you goddam bastard. Alas, poor Jerks or something (I seen that in a play, see? Good line) come on, come on; here's General Pershing come to have a drink with the poor soldiers" (*SP*, p. 9). Yaphank's language here is self-conscious and, despite its colloquial diction, overtly literary—"I seen that in a play, see? Good line." As the section develops (and the soldiers get progressively more drunk) Yaphank's idiolect, with its mixture of personal abuse, ironic misquotation, and absurd military reference, prevails over Lowe's puerile effusions, and the veteran's cynical jibes and rambling non sequiturs quickly become the dominant mode of discourse.

Although consistently humorous in tone, Yaphank's oratorical expansions and conversational retorts frequently return to the fundamental differences between veterans and civilians and he repeatedly, though often obliquely, invokes the newly demobilized soldiers' underlying sense of social displacement and emotional isolation. In this respect, the allusion to the "ancient mariner" in the passage quoted above may not be accidental or insignificant, for Yaphank characteristically portrays the veterans as outcasts or aliens, "unworthy strangers in a foreign land"—no doubt anticipating the initial description of Donald Mahon as a "lost foreigner"; and at one point he even sarcastically suggests that "us soldiers got to stick together in a foreign country like this" (*SP*, p. 10). The episode's violently farcical action tends to underscore this theme, and the soldiers' absurdly staged (and finally reconsidered) attempt to jump from the moving train not only provides a further example of their uncivilized (and uncivilian) behavior but, more importantly, physically separates them from the remainder of the passengers—dramatically symbolizing their alienation and giving narrative substance to Yaphank's sarcastic observations. This dichotomy between civilian and veteran or, perhaps more properly, between representatives of the pre- and post-war world is central to the pattern and meaning of *Soldiers' Pay* as a whole, and as the novel develops and the soldiers' homecoming progressively affects larger areas of society, Faulkner maintains this division and sharply points up the confrontations that result from it.

Section 1 of the first chapter provides an abrupt but effective introduction to these fundamental narrative tensions. And though the almost compulsive heightening of the novel's initial, and most explicitly military, scenes might indeed represent Faulkner's attempt "to establish from the start . . . the credentials of *Soldiers' Pay* as a war novel,"[5] it is significant, particularly in view of his subsequent literary development, that he chose to open this war novel with a stylistic tour de force, subordinating plot or characterization to the exercise of language and the statement of theme. In terms of the work's larger structure, section 1 can be seen to operate almost exclusively as a kind of thematic prologue, delineating the general features of the veterans' social reintegration rather than focusing on any of its specific manifestations. This representative function is emphasized over and above any consideration for character motivation or narrative plausibility.

To call attention to the symbolic activity of the novel's central character, for example, Faulkner not only provides him with a highly figurative mode of discourse but also gives him what is, in effect, a topical pseudonym. By the use of the name Yaphank, suggestive of the whole class of returning "yanks,"[6] Faulkner economically establishes a functional distinction between the broadly drawn, essentially emblematic creature in section 1, and the more carefully delineated, psychologically motivated figure who is reintroduced as Joe Gilligan in section 2. Faulkner perceived that Yaphank, in his role as symbol of the returning soldiers and mouthpiece for their distinctive language, must be differentiated from Gilligan, the character who falls in love with Mrs. Powers and ministers to Donald Mahon (the true symbolic representative of the ravages of war). Faulkner therefore revised the novel's typescript to provide Gilligan with a stage name for use in the exaggerated comedy of the first section.[7]

The conclusion of this highly theatrical farce involves a conventional dramatic reversal, and Yaphank's gambit with the salesmen and the police effectively ensures a comic termination. His clever substitution of the civilians acting as guards (Schluss and his companion) for the drunken veterans in custody (Lowe and himself) not only maintains the episode's burlesque framework but also, and more significantly, reasserts its dominant narrative tensions. The replacement of the civilians—who spout such phrases as "I would of liked to of fought by your side, see?" (*SP*, p. 17)—by the recently discharged soldiers symbolically introduces the veterans' new postwar roles and establishes their orientation toward a problematic future. After leaving the salesmen to the mercies of the police, Yaphank and Lowe are caught "in the magic of change," and, partially shedding their former military identities, "they stood feeling the spring in the cold air, as if they had but recently come into a new world, feeling their littleness and believing too that lying in wait for them was something new and strange" (*SP*, p. 22). This symbolic rebirth provides an appropriate closure for the action in section 1. It also constitutes the termination of the episode's overtly theatrical and figurative style, thus marking it off as a self-contained, rhetorically discrete narrative unit, related to the very different stylistic and rhetorical world of the next section—and indeed to the novel as a whole—almost solely by means of its structural placement.[8]

Similarly abrupt and confusing openings mark a number
of Faulkner's later works, and variations on this technique
operate in *Flags in the Dust*, where Will Falls's jumbled
tale of John Sartoris's civil war escapade begins the narrative, as well as in *The Sound and the Fury*, where the reader
is immediately greeted by the unfamiliar interior world of
Benjy Compson. In *Soldiers' Pay*, however, this initial confusion does not last long, and from section 2 onward, Faulkner adopts a less extravagant style to introduce some of the
major characters, to delineate the postwar social attitudes,
to initiate the general plot, and thus to open the narrative
proper. The idiosyncratic and outmoded language of the war
which controlled part 1 is now replaced by a more familiar,
and more familiarly Faulknerian, expressive medium, and
the general outlines of the "new world" which the soldiers
"had but recently come into" begin to emerge. Linguistic
differences thus come to serve structural functions, and in
moving from the New Orleans prose to *Soldiers' Pay*, it
becomes clear how quickly Faulkner capitalized on his protean stylistic range and united it with his growing conception of a fundamentally broken aesthetic form.

The decisive rhetorical shift between section 1 and the
remainder of the novel can perhaps best be seen in the initial
confrontation between the recently rechristened Gilligan and
Mrs. Powers, a young war widow who boldly joins the
group of soldiers and quickly assumes a dominant role in
the plot. In this scene, Faulkner not only refrains from providing the veteran's verbal reaction to the mysterious "dark
woman" with the "girl's voice" (a narrative gambit that would
have been impossible within the rhetorical context of the
first section) but, in order to characterize her properly, explicitly eschews the soldier's point of view altogether, noting that since Gilligan had never seen a work by Aubrey
Beardsley he could not possibly "have known that Beardsley would have sickened for her: he had drawn her so often

dressed in peacock hues, white and slim and depraved among meretricious trees and impossible marble fountains" (*SP*, p. 31). Although the fin de siècle imagery and the specific allusion to Beardsley most obviously differentiate this passage from the extravagant colloquialisms of section 1, the change in expressive technique involves a variation in narrative perspective as well: an omniscient commentator is introduced, verbal exchanges no longer dominate the presentation, and Mrs. Powers can be portrayed in terms of culturally resonant images strikingly at odds with Yaphank's characteristic mode of discourse.

As the novel develops, the third-person nondramatized narrator becomes increasingly prominent, and various descriptive and rhetorical techniques displace the histrionic confusion of the first section of chapter 1. Mrs. Powers's humble hotel room thus receives a stylized, frankly aesthetic rendering involving visual allusions to cubist or vorticist effects: "she lay staring down the tunnel of her room, watching the impalpable angles of furniture, feeling through plastered smug walls a rumor of spring outside. The airshaft was filled with a prophecy of April come again into the world. Like a heedless idiot into a world that had forgotten Spring. The white connecting door took the vague indication of a transom and held it in a mute and luminous plane" (*SP*, p. 37). A correspondingly high style, replete with archaic diction and classically derived metaphors, is also used to give further elaboration and narrative substantiation to Cadet Lowe's frustrated sense of martial inadequacy. What was defined simply as a "disgusted sorrow" in section 1 is now rhetorically expanded, becoming "all the old sorrows of the Jasons of the world who see their vessels sink ere the harbor is left behind" (*SP*, p. 31). The cultivated narrator also calls portentous abstractions into play: after Lowe meets Donald Mahon—the horribly disfigured aviator who serves as the dominant symbol of the war's devastation[9]—he is depicted as feeling "the comradeship of those whose lives had become pointless through the sheer equivocation of events, of the sorry jade, Circumstance" (*SP*, p. 30).

While this type of traditional omniscient commentary ap pears throughout the novel, *Soldiers' Pay* also provides evidence of Faulkner's further experiments with point of view, and a surprising variety of techniques for presenting inner thoughts and emotions can be found in the first chapter alone. For example, to characterize more fully the somewhat mysterious Mrs. Powers and explain the motivation for her abrupt and almost pathological attraction to Mahon, Faulkner focuses on her consciousness and dramatizes those memories evoked by her personal experience of the hopelessly wounded aviator. Section 3 opens with her alone in a hotel room preparing for "the old familiarity of sleep," her mind filling "with a remembered troubling sadness" as she vividly, but abstractly, recalls Lieutenant Richard Powers, "her husband youngly dead in France" (*SP*, p. 36). Faulkner initially summarizes her brief relationship with Powers through conventional techniques of *erlebte Rede* (not unlike those he had experimented with in "Home" and some of the other New Orleans prose), flatly describing the sexual motives for their marriage—"for the purpose of getting of each other a brief ecstasy"—her subsequent recantation, and her lingering sense of guilt at his having been killed in action before receiving her explanatory letter: "He had not even got her letter! This in some way seemed the infidelity: having him die still believing in her, bored though they both probably were" (*SP*, p. 36).

Despite her bitter sense of loss, Mrs. Powers still feels "that passionate desire to cling to something concrete in a dark world" (*SP*, p. 36), and, "obeying an impulse," she looks in on the sleeping Mahon and "in an instinctive flash" somehow senses his imminent blindness and impending death. Musing on guilt, mutability, and the realities of death, she again recalls her "troubling sadness," but now explicitly associates Mahon with her dead husband. The language here is much more emotionally charged than that of the earlier reminiscence. As psychologically significant self-questioning replaces abstracted memory, thoughts become fragmented, connectives disappear, and the overall method of narrative presentation becomes more directly reflective of the vacillations of a troubled mind. As Mrs. Powers becomes increasingly disturbed, Faulkner thus moves from *erlebte Rede* to more dramatic techniques of interior monologue, providing an ummediated glimpse of her introspective probing. After discussing Mahon's predicament with Joe Gilligan, she asks herself why it was that "you deliberately took certain people to break your intimacy, why these people died, why you yet took others. . . . Will my death be like this: fretting and exasperating? Am I cold by nature, or have I spent all my emotional coppers, that I don't seem to feel things like others? Dick, Dick. Ugly and dead" (*SP*, p. 39; Faulkner's ellipsis).

The final phrase specifically evokes Mrs. Powers's lost husband, but Powers and Mahon have become intermingled in her consciousness. As the chapter develops, this incantatory fragment takes on a broader significance and is progressively transferred to her personal experience of Mahon. To clarify the referential function of this motif and thus stress the association between Powers and Mahon, Faulkner introduces a technique whereby representative images of the two lieutenants are isolated from the narrative and implicitly related through formal juxtaposition: "(Dear dead Dick.) (Mahon under his scar, sleeping.) (Dick, my dearest one.)" (*SP*, p. 44). Although the parenthetical units themselves typographically call attention to the potential correspondences, the frame pattern and overall syntactical organization of the sentences rhetorically insist on the soldiers' interrelation. Gilligan's frank summary and reiteration of

Mrs. Powers's financial decision ("Soldier dies and leaves you money, and you spend the money helping another soldier die comfortable" [*SP*, p. 44]) further underscores this relationship and—by explicitly recalling Mrs. Powers's earlier monetary hint, "I know what I'll do with the insurance" (*SP*, p. 36)—indicates the degree to which her ambiguous emotional attachment to Mahon involves deliberate self-sacrifice and personal expiation.

By the end of this section, prompted by her acute awareness of Mahon's condition and her newly reawakened memories of her husband's death, Mrs. Powers feels totally disassociated from her immediate surroundings; her "smug, impersonal room" seems "like an appointed tomb . . . high above a world of joy and sorrow and lust for living" (*SP*, p. 44). The episode concludes with a deeply emotional and intensely personal interior monologue, differentiated in language, tone, and technique from the calm and somewhat ironic abstractions that opened the section. Now her imagination fills with brutally antithetical images evoking mutability and physical corruption; the pain and utter discontinuity of death is expressed in violently concrete terms: "(Dick, Dick. Dead, ugly Dick. Once you were alive and young and passionate and ugly, after a time you were dead, dear Dick: that flesh, that body, which I loved and did not love; your beautiful, young, ugly body, dear Dick, become now a seething of worms, like new milk. Dear Dick.)" (*SP*, p. 44).

By focusing sharply on Mrs. Powers's consciousness and presenting the dynamics of her increasingly intense and revelatory confrontations with the sufferings of her past, Faulkner not only delineates the psychological basis for her attraction to Mahon, but also, and perhaps more importantly for the design of the novel, establishes the wounded aviator's broadly symbolic function—demonstrating his ability to elicit and represent profoundly personal reactions to the devastation of the war. As Mahon approaches death and the pattern of symbolic reference broadens, Mrs. Powers's obsessively repeated phrase ("Dick, ugly Dick") joins other such fragments that have come to be associated with the aviator (such as the rector's "This is my son. He is dead.") and thus falls into place within the elaborate network of recurrent motifs that serves to define his representative role.

As if to add yet another technique to his growing expressive repertoire, Faulkner presents Cadet Lowe's hopelessly naive reaction to Mahon by means of quite a different narrative strategy. For Lowe, Mahon does not represent the violent discontinuities and devastation caused by the war, but rather symbolizes a goal, the sublime peak of adolescent intoxication not so much with war itself but with the romantic gestures (including being horribly wounded) made possible by war. To illustrate and evaluate this anachronistic attitude—"the old bunk about knights of the air and the romance of battle," as Gilligan puts it (*SP*, p. 41)—Faulkner creates a rhetorical pattern whereby Lowe's consciousness is focused on directly and his envious assessments of Mahon's military "achievement" are contrasted with more objective descriptions of the flyer's condition. Lowe's uncontrollable physical revulsion to Mahon's "dreadful scar" ("My God he thought, turning sick") is juxtaposed to his jealous dream: "Had I been old enough or lucky enough, this might have been me" (*SP*, p. 25). His fatuous fantasy "(Would I sleep? thought Lowe; had I wings, boots, would I sleep?)" (*SP*, p. 30) is similarly set against descriptions of Mahon's pathetic mental affliction—his profoundly "puzzled and distracted" gaze—and Gilligan's frighteningly sober reaction to it: "My God, it makes you sick at the stomach, don't it?" (*SP*, p. 29).

As the chapter develops and the reader learns more about the seriousness of Mahon's condition, Lowe's narrative perspective becomes more prominent and his self-indulgent comparisons with Mahon become ever more pointedly ironic. This pattern reaches a climax in the chapter's penultimate section, which is presented almost entirely from Lowe's point of view and concludes with a pathetically envious comparison: "To have been him! he moaned. Just to be him. Let him take this sound body of mine! Let him take it. To have got wings on my breast, to have wings; and to have got his scar, too, I would take death to-morrow" (*SP*, p. 45). Similar, though perhaps less strident, techniques of dramatic irony are employed throughout the novel to characterize and criticize Cecily Saunders, George Farr, Januarius Jones, and the postwar youth in general. But although Lowe has much in common with these figures, he primarily serves a more limited and topical narrative function. Once his excessively romantic attitudes to the war have been adequately exposed in the first chapter, his role is fulfilled and he thereafter disappears from the text—except as the author of a similarly ironic series of letters.[10]

In chapter 1 the reader thus witnesses a broad range of rhetorical strategies and narrative techniques, a formal virtuosity approaching that of the deliberately experimental *Times-Picayune* prose, forever moving toward that standard of mobility and plasticity envisioned by Wright. Yet that first chapter's structural and linguistic diversity only begins to indicate the overall expressive heterogeneity of *Soldiers' Pay*. As the novel proceeds, Faulkner introduces other styles and techniques to portray different aspects of the "new" postwar world and, through their juxtaposition, ultimately creates a polyvocal structure that exploits the interaction of various and often disparate modes of fictional discourse.

In chapter 2, for example, the rector's carefully cultivated garden is described in a highly ornate, allusive, and fundamentally derivative expressive medium that is much closer in language and tone to *The Marble Faun* or sections of the contemporaneous "New Orleans" than to even the most elaborately wrought segments of chapter 1: "Beyond the oaks, against a wall of poplars in a restless formal row were columns of a Greek temple, yet the poplars themselves in slim, vague green were poised and vain as girls in a frieze. Against a privet hedge would soon be lilies like nuns in a cloister and blue hyacinths swung soundless bells, dreaming of Lesbos. Upon a lattice wall wistaria would soon burn in slow inverted lilac flame, and following it they came lastly upon a single rose bush. The branches were huge and knotted with age, heavy and dark as a bronze pedestal, crowned with pale impermanent gold" (*SP*, p. 61).[11]

The tendency of the similes to move from the natural to the aesthetic ("poplars . . . poised and vain as girls in a frieze," lilies like nuns in a cloister," "branches . . . heavy and dark as a bronze pedestal"), the deliberately stylized pictorial images ("inverted lilac flame," "branches . . . crowned with pale impermanent gold"), and the conventional classical echoes ("columns of a Greek temple," "dreaming of Lesbos") evoke the artificiality of the formal garden—a symbol of, among other things, the rector's abstraction and emotional withdrawal. Similar and similarly rendered gardens, as critics have pointed out, had appeared in earlier works, most notably in *The Marble Faun* and in *The Marionettes*.[12] But although the excessively "poeticized" description in *Soldiers' Pay* reveals certain continuities, it more clearly reveals growth and change. In the previous texts, fin de siècle mannerisms completely dominated; there was no stylistic variation. Everything was presented through this type of discourse and hence colored by late-romantic linguistic conventions. If the setting was perceived as being dreamy, static, and beyond time, so was the marble faun himself and Pierrot—and so, more damagingly, was the faun's "escape" and Pierrot's and Marietta's passion.

Between writing these texts and writing *Soldiers' Pay* Faulkner learned that this voice was merely one of his voices, not his only voice, and he uses it in the novel specifically to depict the postwar world's first spring and thus provide the appropriate atmosphere and temporal setting for Mahon's Lazarus-like return. Thus, in scenes that center on the effects of Mahon's homecoming, natural phenomena become vaguely emblematic images of stasis: "At the corner of the house was a tree covered with tiny white-bellied leaves like a mist, like a swirl of arrested silver water" (*SP*, p. 109). Landscapes are likewise presented through elaborate strings of stylized similes: "At last the reddened edge of the disc was sliced like a cheese by the wistaria-covered lattice wall and the neutral buds were a pale agitation against the dead afternoon. Soon the evening star would be there above the poplar tip, perplexing it, immaculate and ineffable, and the poplar was vain as a girl darkly in an arrested passionate ecstacy. Half of the moon was a coin broken palely near the zenith and at the end of the lawn the first fireflies were like lazily blown sparks from cool fires" (*SP*, p. 286).

Characters receive similar treatment, and Faulkner typically defines certain figures in terms of stock mythological epithets. Thus, throughout the novel, Jones is repeatedly described as a "satyr" with "yellow" or "goat's eyes," whose "face was a round mirror before which fauns and nymphs might have wantoned when the world was young" (*SP*, p. 58); Cecily is seen as a "young poplar," or as a "Hamadryad, a slim jeweled one" (*SP*, p. 77); while the prewar Mahon is recollected as a "faun," though now he more closely resembles a "marble faun," physically immobile and restricted to the confines of a carefully cultivated garden.

During the course of the novel, as the seasons move from spring to early summer, these recurring classical epithets become related to the sequence of stylized nature images, and together they create an evocative texture of literary and mythical allusion. Set against this deliberately resonant style are presentations of Mahon's slow death, and a symbolically suggestive pattern is created, which some critics believe to be informed by Frazer's *The Golden Bough*, Eliot's *The Waste Land*, Freud's *Beyond the Pleasure Principle*, or even, possibly, a more all-embracing Christian/pagan dialectic.[13] Thus, on one level of patterning, satyrs and nymphs celebrate the dance of the seasons, while at another, static images of decadence and futility disrupt the revels and prepare the context for the wounded hero's relentless motion toward "division and death." Despite the multiple layers of intricately woven echoes and allusions, Faulkner does not create a functional framework of mythical correspondences, and his use of these motifs tends to reflect his awareness and absorption of contemporary literary mannerisms rather than any attempt to build an integrated or comprehensive symbolic structure.

Given the almost obsessive borrowing that marked Faulkner's earlier imaginative productions—given, too, his demonstrable familiarity with Swinburne, Housman, Beardsley, Nichols and the English decadents, as well as his knowledge of such self-conscious prose stylists as Walter Pater, Joseph Hergesheimer, Thomas Beer, James Branch Cabell, and John Cowper Powys—it is hardly surprising that portions of *Soldiers' Pay* should exhibit a deliberate attempt at ornate stylization and display the characteristic diction, rhythm, syntax, and imagery of late-romantic forms. Although this particular medium is derivative in a general sense—many of Faulkner's favorite fin de siècle formulas had become widely used literary stereotypes by the early twenties—there are verifiable sources for a number of the novel's individual passages (such as the allusions to Edward Fitzgerald's version of the *Rubáiyát of Omar Khayyám* in the final chapter)[14] as well as for some of its character types. And, even at this stage, Faulkner continued his imitative appropriation of available literary conventions.

Although, according to one early reviewer, "Januarius

Jones undoubtedly dropped from the moon,"[15] later critics
have shown that this goatlike, poetry-spouting sybarite and
his sexual sparring partner, Cecily Saunders, have more
immediate antecedents in James Branch Cabell's *Jurgen* and
in the art of Aubrey Beardsley.[16] It is also very possible that
Faulkner's depiction of Jones and Cecily owes something to
Aldous Huxley's *Crome Yellow*, in which a young woman
is specifically described as a "Hamadryad of the poplar sap-
ling," a "slim Hamadryad whose movements were like the
swaying of a young tree in the wind,"[17] and in which the
narrator ironically comments on youthful flirtation with precisely the same biblical quotation (Gen. 1:27) that Faulkner
uses to epitomize Jones's characteristic lust: "Male and female created He them" (*SP*, p. 314).[18]

Examination of some other stylistically distinct sections
of the novel reveals a similar, if less extensive, dependence
on fictional models. In chapter 5, for example, where ironically juxtaposed episodes of war and peace bring the text's
central evaluative contrasts into high relief, Faulkner focuses for the first time on battlefield action and, at one point,
describes the initial advance of a company of recruits: "At
last they were going in themselves after a measureless space
of aimless wandering here and there, and the sound of guns
though seemingly no nearer was no longer impersonal. They
tramped by night, feeling their feet sink, then hearing them
suck in mud. Then they felt sloping ground and were in a
ditch. It was as if they were burying themselves, descending
into their own graves in the bowels of the wet black earth,
into a darkness so dense as to constrict breathing, constrict
the heart. They stumbled on in the darkness" (*SP*, p. 177).
It is apparent that the overall style and tone of this passage
is quite remote from the aesthetic formalism of the garden
scenes, as well as from the theatrical chaos of chapter 1.
Unlike the artificial landscapes, the imagery here is not solely
visual, and the descriptive language is based on a broad

range of sensory impressions: the recruits hear the "sound of guns" and the "suck" of their feet in the mud; they feel "their feet sink" and experience the "sloping ground" despite "a darkness so dense as to constrict breathing, constrict the heart." The controlling simile ("It was as if they were burying themselves, descending into their own graves in the bowels of the wet black earth") also revolves around personal perceptions and derives its effect from psychological rather than literary correspondences. The ubiquitous mud, the tactile and aural imagery, the experiential simile, and the persistent use of the plural pronoun (emphasizing the squad's common perceptions) all contribute to a concrete presentation of the sensations of the front-line troops.

Since Faulkner's military career was spent on Canadian airfields, this vivid and convincing depiction of combat owes more to literary sources than to personal experience. Lacking direct knowledge of the war, it is hardly surprising that he should draw on his reading and employ secondary materials to eke out the resources of his imagination. In "Literature and War," a roughly contemporaneous essay which remained unpublished until 1973, Faulkner provides a brief, though extremely suggestive, inventory and assessment of this reading, acknowledging a familiarity with such figures as Siegfried Sassoon, Henri Barbusse, Rupert Brooke, and R. H. Mottram.[19] The essay, however, not only identifies a number of contemporary authors and texts with which Faulkner was acquainted, it also, through its intermittently parodic style, demonstrates his remarkable ability to assimilate his influences, and thus points toward the particular motifs and techniques that he appropriated to portray action in the trenches. Like the New Orleans prose exercises, "Literature and War" functions as a kind of workshop for the creative exploration of the war idiom, and by the time he wrote the essay, Faulkner had already absorbed a number of the war literature's dominant rhetorical formulas. In the first

paragraph, for example, he replicates Sassoon's characteristic subject matter and imagery and transmutes it into an
evocative depiction of life at the front. The concentration
on the pervasive damp, together with the exclusive focus
on the soldiers' sensory impressions ("heard and felt them
sqush [sic] and suck in the mud . . . seen the casual dead . . .
smelt that dreadful smell of war"),[20] thus anticipates the
combat episodes in Soldiers' Pay, while calling attention to
their specific literary antecedents.

Critics of Soldiers' Pay have mentioned not only Cabell,
Beardsley, and the writers of the war, but also such formidable artists as Joyce, Eliot, Conrad, Woolf, and, of course,
Sherwood Anderson in discussing some of the novel's specific stylistic models.[21] Indeed, the range of influence in
Soldiers' Pay is, perhaps, no less remarkable than Faulkner's ability to absorb it creatively. Alongside passages reflecting the English decadents, the war poets, or the moderns,
one discovers debts to more popular, contemporary figures.
The parody of "smart" journalism in chapter 5 (SP, pp.
188–89), for instance, is unlikely to have been written in
ignorance of the mannerisms of such modish writers as Sin-
clair Lewis, H. L. Mencken, and George Ade. And it seems
likely, as Hugh Kenner has recently argued, that the impulse
to distinguish separate narrative materials by obvious linguistic variation may be the most important lesson Faulkner
learned from his "sampling" of Ulysses.[22]

The use of other technical devices appears to be similarly
derivative. In section 2 of chapter 3 (SP, pp. 100–101), for
example, Faulkner delays narrative disclosure and heightens
expectation by withholding a definite description of the particular "object" young Robert Saunders carries until the very
moment when "it"—the flashlight—is "snapped on." Although this rather simple rhetorical technique is not limited
to any one author or text, it is apparent that Faulkner appropriated it from the opening episode of Joseph Hergeshei-

mer's *The Bright Shawl*, especially since Faulkner himself points out Hergesheimer's "skilful" use of this particular "trick of the trade" in his early review: "The induction to The Bright Shawl is good—he talks of the shawl for a page or so before one is aware of the presence of the shawl as a material object, before the word itself is said" (*EP*, p. 102).[23]

In *Soldiers' Pay*, such "stealing"—to use Faulkner's term— whether of language or technique, was carried out in response to specific compositional needs.[24] Unlike the earlier apprentice imitations, which involved wholesale appropriations of style and strategies, Faulkner was here learning what all developing artists must learn—to pick and choose from existing expressive conventions. He was also, and more importantly, learning how to transmute and imaginatively digest these conventions. In the combat passage quoted above, for example, Faulkner makes the borrowed materials characteristically his own by embedding them in a prose medium built largely of negatives ("no nearer . . . no longer impersonal"), abstract adjectives ("measureless space"), syntactical repetitions ("constrict the breathing, constrict the heart"), and heavy subordination (the penultimate sentence). Although other influences are not so successfully absorbed, *Soldiers' Pay* shows Faulkner attempting to come to terms with them and, perhaps even more significantly, with the larger process of creative assimilation through which all artists must eventually pass.

Soldiers' Pay, at the same time, shows Faulkner continuing his more personal experiments in language, style, and narrative patterning—as the radically inventive mode of the novel's opening section sufficiently indicates. Taken as whole, in fact, this text is as exploratory as it is derivative. Faulkner introduces, for instance, an interesting and singular technique to chronicle the more far-reaching effects of Donald Mahon's homecoming. As the action of the novel radiates outward from the rector's garden and affects ever-wider areas

of Charlestown society, Faulkner supplements omniscient
summary narration with a "town voice." This anonymous
voice appears at various points in the text and dramatically
articulates corporate responses to the central plot through
the characteristic linguistic mannerisms of the local community. In chapter 8 Faulkner employs this voice to present
an ironic summary of the action in terms of the dominant
society's clearly defined value structure: "Besides, it was all
legal now. Miss Cecily Saunders was safely married—though
nobody knows where they was from the time they drove out
of town in George Farr's car until they was properly married
by a priest in Atlanta the next day (but then I always told
you about that girl). . . . And that Mrs. What's-her-name,
that tall black-headed woman at Mahon's, had at last married someone"(*SP*, p. 281).

The corporate voice captures the ethos of the Charlestown
community and, though much less ambitious in scope or
narrative function, it also anticipates similar experiments
with a collective consciousness in Faulkner's more mature
works, including such socially representative narrators as
Cora Tull or Chick Mallison. "The Town," in fact, works
almost as a dramatized narrator in *Soldiers' Pay*, and in
those highly experimental sections of the novel where repeated phrases and motifs are juxtaposed within a playlike
format, "The Town" appears among the dramatis personae
and offers observations along with the other characters:

The Town:
That girl . . . time she was took in hand by somebody. Run-
ning around town nearly nekkid. Good thing he's blind, ain't it?
Guess she hopes he'll stay blind, too. . . .

Margaret Powers:
No, no, good-bye, dear dead Dick, ugly dead Dick. . . .

Joe Gilligan:
He is dying, he gets the woman he doesn't want even, while

I am not dying. . . . Margaret, what shall I do? What can I say?

Emmy:
Come here, Emmy? Ah, come to me, Donald. But he is dead.

Cecily Saunders:
George, my lover, my poor dear. . . . What have we done?

[*SP*, pp. 262–63; Faulkner's ellipses][25]

Other distinctive techniques in the novel are less obviously adventurous. In chapter 3, section 8, for example, Faulkner introduces a deceptively simple narrative strategy to evoke Emmy's past, especially her prewar relationship with Mahon. The basic material for Emmy's almost self-contained narrative is clearly derived from an earlier short story, "Adolescence," which depicts a very similar backwoods romance.[26] Although Faulkner drew heavily on this story for the characterization of the two young people, the setting, and the central action, the particular quality and significance of Emmy's tale lies more in its distinctive narrative mode than in its subject matter or pattern of incident. In the novel, unlike the short story, Faulkner exploits the "inarticulate" girl's expressive limitations to create a strikingly fresh and artless narrative voice that emphasizes the healthy, animal-like innocence of the love affair.

Emmy's descriptive language is based solely on her sensations and impressions and is hence innocent of literary formulas and stock rhetorical devices. She views Mahon, not as a faun, but as one who "ought to live in the woods"(*SP*, p. 125), perceives "the moonlight kind of running on his wet shoulders and arms," and feels "like a bird, kind of: like you was going swooping right away from the ground or something" (*SP*, p. 127). Her primitive diction, simplistic comparisons, and childlike evocations of nature create a quasi-pastoral atmosphere so that her narrative, taken as a whole, functions as a kind of idyll in the midst of the developing wasteland, representing lost possibilities and recalling a wholesome ingenuousness that the postwar world has forgotten.[27] This interpolated story, with its linguistically naive narrator and its emphasis on communion with the natural processes, shows Faulkner beginning to work with a fictional style that he would develop further in later novels and that anticipates the creation of the powerful nature hymns in such works as *The Hamlet* and *Go Down, Moses*.

Although a number of these individual prose styles and rhetorical strategies point toward Faulkner's more mature work, certain aspects of this first novel reflect his brief literary past. Critics have noticed the way in which he reuses material from "The Cobbler" in the characterization of the rector,[28] how the protagonist of "The Lilacs" serves as a prototype for Donald Mahon,[29] and the extent to which certain images and phrases derive from his verse explorations.[30] Noteworthy too in this connection is the reliance on "Moonlight," another early short story, for the portrayal of Cecily Saunders and George Farr and the depiction of their troubled romance.[31] In general, however, *Soldiers' Pay* owes more to *The Marble Faun* than to any other of Faulkner's previous literary productions. The novel exhibits the reworking of some of the poem's motifs; it also, more importantly, shares its characteristic patterning and basic structural methodology. *Soldiers' Pay*, like *The Marble Faun*, remains a fundamentally broken text: the nine chapters are divided into numerous subsections and short dramatic scenes, which frequently function as self-contained formal units, very much like the individual lyrics that comprise the poem. The novel's typescript provides confirmatory evidence for this structure and shows Faulkner radically shifting autonomous blocks of material and significantly altering patterns of scenic juxtaposition. Thus, at one stage of composition, the novel opened in the rector's garden, and Emmy's prewar pastoral was a distinct narrative episode entitled "In the Kitchen"; in different drafts chapter 9 appeared as either chapter 5 or 8.[32] As shown above, significant stylistic differences further distinguish and separate these individual sections, and by organizing his aesthetic whole to exploit the interaction of these discrete verbal and narrative parts, Faulkner first examined those principles of design that would eventually inform the more radically discontinuous structures of such works as *The Sound and the Fury*.

Given a similarity of underlying formal conception in *The Marble Faun* and *Soldiers' Pay*, it is not surprising that Faulkner resorted to comparable organizational strategies. His attempt to integrate and harmonize this deliberately fragmented and polyvocal text reflects structural procedures that inform the earlier poem. Not only is there the same emphasis on seasonal progression and mythical reference, there is also a corresponding reliance on resonating patterns of recurrent images and motifs. One repeatedly finds woven throughout the novel phrases such as "pigeons remote and unemphatic as sleep" or "pigeons . . . like smears of paint" (*SP*, pp. 104, 170, 180, 181, 184, 279) and evocations of the emblematic tree with its "white-bellied leaves" (*SP*, pp. 109, 247, 252, 254, 272, 281). Certain narrative relationships are also implied by means of rhetorically heightened image reiteration. For example, the identification of Mrs. Burney's son Dewey with the soldier who killed Mrs. Powers's husband is indicated solely by means of the emphatic repetition of the combat scene describing the officer's death on the "fire-step" (*SP*, pp. 179, 186, 211, 262).

The Marble Faun's overall temporal design and its pattern of formal juxtaposition, however, most clearly anticipate the structural method of *Soldiers' Pay*.[33] Even though fragmented time schemes and narrative montage are characteristic of much modern fiction,[34] the use of temporal parallelism

in *Soldiers' Pay* seems to reflect a more personal structural
approach, especially since Faulkner had already successfully employed a similar formal strategy to organize the
individual sections of his pastoral poem. In any case, the
depiction of simultaneous action is an important element of
narrative presentation in *Soldiers' Pay*, and Faulkner introduces this technique, as he did in *The Marble Faun*, principally to interrelate and evaluate distinct rhetorical units.
In order, for example, to fuse the disconnected and fundamentally disparate fictional worlds of chapters 1 and 2,
Faulkner juxtaposes two significant series of incidents—
Donald Mahon's arrival at Charlestown and Cecily Saunders's meeting with George Farr—so that their simultaneous
occurrence is exaggerated and rhetorically heightened. The
juxtaposition compels the reader to view these scenes together and to perceive their interrelations in terms of the
novel's larger evaluative framework, and thus it distinctly
anticipates the development of more sophisticated techniques of simultaneity, such as the parallel presentation of
the Easter service and Jason's search for Quentin at the
conclusion of *The Sound and the Fury*.

In *Soldiers' Pay* Faulkner carefully prepares the context
for this narrative alignment, so that by the end of the second
chapter the reader is well aware of the moral, symbolic, and
linguistic dichotomy that separates the soldiers who have
served (and Mrs. Powers) from the postwar youth. As the
first chapter makes clear, Mahon's homecoming works symbolically and, like the initial scenes of the soldiers' Pullman
theatrics, helps to epitomize the veterans' difficult social
reintegration. The wounded aviator's homeward journey not
only dramatizes his personal destiny but, through Mrs.
Powers's identification of him with her dead husband, also
becomes representative of her private search for expiation;
similarly, because Gilligan's incipient relationship with Mrs.
Powers opens possibilities for their romantic union, it si-

multaneously becomes a potential vehicle for his resumption of civilian life. Furthermore, since Mahon's family and friends in Charlestown believe him to be dead, his "resurrection" (in chapter 2) disrupts their complacency and forces them, at least temporarily, to confront the returning veterans and acknowledge the complicated problems of peace.

In terms of plot, chapter 1 emphasizes the importance of Mahon's prewar engagement to Cecily Saunders (*SP*, pp. 29–30, 40–43) and suggests that its smooth resumption might perhaps bridge the profound gap created by the devastation of the war, providing an act of affirmation for those who, according to Gilligan, "want to believe that something in his world ain't turned upside down" (*SP*, p. 41). Cecily's initial portrait in chapter 2, however, leaves little hope for an early or successful reunion. The jeweled "Hamadryad" is as "graceful and insincere as a French sonnet" (*SP*, p. 71), quite a distance, morally and rhetorically, from Mahon's "terrible face," "dreadful scar," and "withered hand." When Cecily learns of Mahon's homecoming, her characteristically flirtatious posture remains unchanged;[35] and though she self-consciously reiterates her love for Mahon ("rubbing herself like a cat on the rector's arm" [*SP*, p. 83]), at the sound of an automobile horn she rushes outside to meet her present boyfriend, George Farr. While the couple drives away from the Mahons' house, the narrator includes an apparently insignificant detail, "a face in the window, a round face" (*SP*, p. 86), and then goes on to describe the couple's tearful encounter. At this point—four pages after Cecily and George have left the house—Faulkner breaks the text and begins a new section with: "Jones at the window saw them drive away. His round face was enigmatic" (*SP*, p. 89). The repeated image of the "round face," together with the typographical gap between the sections, serves as a transitional device that takes the reader back to an earlier moment in the narrative and picks up the action from there. A nonconsecutive temporal relationship exists between this and the previous section—the events of this episode (sec. 5) in fact happen during the same period as the lovers' meeting (sec. 4). Since the action in section 5 occurs inside of the rector's house and concerns the assembled group's preparations to meet Donald Mahon's train, the moment of the veteran's homecoming is thus carefully juxtaposed with Cecily's tryst, and the narrative commentary twice reinforces the simultaneity of these events: "The divine became aware of the absence of Cecily, who was at that moment sitting in a stationary motor car in an obscure lane, crying on the shoulder of a man whose name was not Donald" (*SP*, p. 89). Again, a sentence later: "The rector stated fretfully that Cecily, who was at that moment kissing a man whose name was not Donald, should not have gone away at that time" (*SP*, p. 89). By so rigorously insisting on the concurrence of these scenes, Faulkner is doing more than merely ensuring an ironic interpretation of Cecily's behavior. Since the action at the station is not presented, the overall effect of this rhetorical strategy is to replace what "ought" to have been Mahon's crucial reunion with his fiancée by a love scene that subverts any attempt at a meaningful reunion—to displace the homecoming's temporal and narrative space in favor of its antithesis.

The presentation of simultaneous action in *Soldiers' Pay* also serves more specific narrative functions. In the final chapter, for example, Faulkner introduces a more innovative technique of temporal alignment in order to draw two of the novel's dominant lines of action into an effective and mutually reflexive dénouement. In the first section of chapter 9, Donald Mahon's funeral—the final and inevitable outcome of his homecoming—is juxtaposed with Januarius Jones's surprising, but not totally unanticipated, seduction of Emmy. The two strands of plot are correlated through the alternation of short paragraphs describing Jones's behavior with parenthetical passages depicting Mahon's burial. Here, in contrast to the example previously discussed, the spatially distinct events are not superimposed at a single point of narrative tension but are suspended over time. In this way, a reference to "Jones, lurking across the street" immediately precedes a short, parenthetical description of the "uniformed self-constituted guard" marching with Mahon's bier—which, in turn, precedes a further elaboration of Jones's amorous quest (*SP*, p. 295). The typographical arrangement and rapid juxtaposition of these independent lines of action compel the reader to view them together and, as the double sequence of incidents unfolds, an effective structure of contextual relationship emerges.

In the final chapter's opening paragraph, the narrator discursively establishes a natural, even organic, relationship between sex and death: "Sex and death: the front door and the back door of the world. How indissolubly are they associated in us! In youth they lift us out of the flesh, in old age they reduce us again to the flesh; one to fatten us, the other to flay us, for the worm" (*SP*, p. 295). As Jones steadily approaches, Emmy's personal experience of Mahon becomes openly associated with these paired themes. Donald's loss pervades her world: "There was no sound in the kitchen save a clock. Life. Death. Life. Death. Life. Death. Forever and ever" (*SP*, p. 296). And the specific recollection of that special "night long, long ago" when they were lovers is reintroduced through passages that separate "her Donald" (who "was dead long, long ago") from the dying, and now dead, veteran who returned from the war (*SP*, p. 297).

The primitive innocence she experienced with "her Donald" in the prewar idyll, however, has now become soiled by the pain and disillusionment of his homecoming, and the healthy imagery of water and fluidity previously associated with their relationship is now replaced by a crude and somewhat comic image of frigidity: while the funeral "procession moved beneath arching iron letters," Emmy feels "something frozen in her chest, like a dish-cloth in winter" (*SP*, p. 297). Before Mahon's burial, similar negative images of ice and dehydration dominate: the funeral flowers are "stale," and Emmy hears the "dusty cry of sparrows" while repeatedly lamenting "If I could only cry."[36]

At the very moment when the funeral service begins, however, Emmy feels a "touch on her shoulder": "It was a dream! she thought and the frozen dish-rag in her chest melted with unbearable relief, becoming tears. It was Jones who had touched her, but anyone would have been the same and she turned in a passion of weeping, clinging to him" (*SP*, p. 297). The description of this embrace immediately precedes the minister's opening lines "(I am the Resurrection and the Life, saith the Lord. . . .)" and initiates the presentation of their lovemaking in parallel with the burial service. This juxtaposition, together with the dishcloth simile and the satirical reference to the cemetery gate,[37] forcibly undercuts the traditional meaning of the religious ceremony and dramatically reveals that even Emmy's love for Mahon, the one thing that seemed to be of permanent value, is now reduced to a mere sexual want capable of being supplied even by Jones. At the same time the prayer's promise of eternal life is delivered—"(. . . yet shall he live. And whosoever liveth and believeth in Me shall never die. . .)"— Jones kisses Emmy, who "knew no sensation save that of warmth and languorous contentment" (*SP*, p. 297). The religious service is thus seen as mildly farcical, love is shown to be "reduced again to the flesh," and the lascivious satyr appears triumphant: "First she wets my pants, then my coat. But this time she'll dry it for me, or I'll know the reason why" (*SP*, p. 297).

The remainder of the concluding chapter presents a series

of equally bleak, if less sophisticated, narrative closures. The painful "facts of division and death" (*SP*, p. 318) ultimately affect all of the major characters, and their final portraits are characterized by a profound sense of frustration and loss: Gilligan and Mrs. Powers (or Mrs. Mahon) become permanently separated, in apparent disregard of their true feelings; George and Cecily find little satisfaction in their recent honeymoon; Emmy "sorrowfully" returns to the scene of her youthful romance; Jones, still chasing Emmy, remains similarly unfulfilled; and the rector, denied the return of his son once again, reenters "some dream within himself" (*SP*, p. 282). The actual termination of the novel, like the depiction of Mahon's funeral, is not executed at the level of representative action, and Faulkner—as he had done before and was to do so often again—resorts to a poetic finale in order to bring the disparate materials into a final resolution.

The typescript of *Soldiers' Pay* indicates the difficulty he had in formulating this conclusion, and there exist numerous versions of the final scenes.[38] Although some of these alternative endings include material that never appeared in the published text—such as extended interior monologues reiterating the specific details of Gilligan's and the rector's sense of loss—practically all of them terminate with an evocation of a black church service, very similar to the one that in fact concludes the novel:

> Feed Thy Sheep, O Jesus. The voices rose full and soft. There was no organ; no organ was needed as above the harmonic passion of bass and baritone soared a clear soprano of women's voices like a flight of gold and heavenly birds. They stood together in the dust, the rector in his shapeless black, and Gilligan in his new hard serge, listening, seeing the shabby church become beautiful with mellow longing, passionate and sad. Then the singing died, fading away along the mooned

land inevitable with to-morrow and sweat, with sex and death
and damnation; and they turned townward under the moon,
feeling dust in their shoes. [*SP*, p. 319]

This passage fuses images of apotheosis and aesthetic transcendence ("soared a clear soprano of women's voices like
a flight of gold and heavenly birds"; "the shabby church
became beautiful with mellow longing, passionate and sad")
with resonant abstractions, invoking larger and more universally significant areas of experience ("inevitable with to-
morrow and sweat, with sex and death and damnation").
The ending is thus generated by linguistic and rhetorical
intensity rather than by terminal action or thematic statement. By means of this poetical flight, the novel's almost
unrelieved movement toward negation and disillusionment
is halted just short of despair. This alternating positive/neg-
ative closural pattern points forward to such ambitious and
ambiguous verbal conclusions as those of *Flags in the Dust*
and *The Sound and the Fury*, as well as backward to such
obvious technical experiments as "The Hill," "Peter," and
"Frankie and Johnny."

In a 1933 introduction for *The Sound and the Fury* (not
published until 1972), Faulkner retrospectively assessed his
first novel, specifically relating its composition to his larger
aesthetic development: "I had learned a little about writing
from Soldiers' Pay—how to approach language, words: not
with seriousness so much, as an essayist does, but with a
kind of alert respect, as you approach dynamite; even with
joy, as you approach women: perhaps with the same secretly
unscrupulous intentions."[39] Whatever the "secretly unscrupulous intentions," Faulkner's overall "approach to language" in *Soldiers' Pay* marks a considerable advance over
that of his contemporaneous prose exercises. In the process
of developing a narrative structure, he transcended the merely
experimental and allowed style and technique to grow nat-

urally out of his materials. The different linguistic media employed show Faulkner's deliberate pursuit of variation, his striving toward what Wright had termed "true style"— the "ability to change one's manner at random so as to harmonise the expression with the thing expressed."[40]

But if Faulkner learned how to approach language in *Soldiers' Pay*, he also learned how to approach extended narrative form. The fictional patterns that inform this work, though sometimes extravagant and overly self-conscious, reflect seminal attitudes toward structure and design that reappear in future texts and become an increasingly important component of his art. By breaking the narrative into self-contained, stylistically distinct structural units, organizing them primarily by juxtaposition (rather than on traditional causal or sequential principles), and integrating them by recurrent motifs, Faulkner can be seen as developing for the first time his highly personal approach to fictional form, which would find its most successful realization three years later in *The Sound and the Fury*. In *Soldiers' Pay* the characteristic pattern of Faulkner's imaginative growth once again involves repetition and invention, the establishment of a creative relationship between his past and his future. The book thus becomes not only an engaging and effective first novel but also, despite its inconsistencies and lapses, a formidable literary achievement, one that more clearly and closely anticipates the structural organization and formal adventurousness of *The Sound and the Fury* than any of the books written in between.

4.
Variations without Progress
From *Soldiers' Pay* to *Mosquitoes*

In July 1925, having submitted the typescript of *Soldiers' Pay* to Boni and Liveright, Faulkner left New Orleans and embarked on his twice-postponed trip to Europe. He was an avid and observant tourist, as his letters home amply demonstrate, yet sightseeing only occupied a part of his time. During his six months in New Orleans, the young poet had become a committed and energetic writer of fiction, and the pleasant distractions of the continent did little to diminish the size and range of his literary output. Although he occasionally composed a poem while in Europe, prose forms now completely dominated his creative life, and in the four months following his departure he began two novels, mailed four additional sketches to the *Times-Picayune*,[1] drafted "a series of travel things," a "fairy tale," "a queer short story about a case of reincarnation," and continued his experimentation with fictional modes, attempting, among other things, to write poetry "in prose form" (*L*, pp. 9–31 passim).

Soon after arriving in Paris, Faulkner excitedly reported to his mother that he was "in the middle of another novel, a grand one," explaining that he had "put the 'Mosquito' one aside" because he did not feel that he was "quite old enough to write it as it should be written"; he did not "know quite enough about people." The new novel, entitled "Elmer," apparently did not require the wide-ranging experience that was necessary for the completion of the discarded "Mosquito," and Faulkner optimistically predicted that he would finish it within three months. At first the novel went "elegantly well," despite competition from some additional minor projects, among them a "few articles," an "amusing travelogue," and a "beautiful" short story "about the Luxembourg gardens and death." Faulkner then left Paris for a tour of southern France and England, leaving the novel "temporarily," as he wrote to his mother, in order "to begin a new one" (*L*, pp. 13–25 passim). This temporary abandonment, however, soon became permanent, and although he picked up "Elmer" again on his return to Paris, even drastic restructuring failed to revive the work, and with 31,000 words written, he put it away unfinished.[2]

Years later Faulkner said that he had not completed the novel simply because it was not funny enough, and though an examination of the surviving typescript certainly corroborates this judgment, it also reveals that the author encountered more fundamental imaginative problems.[3] Basically, it appears that "Elmer" was intended to be a kind of satiric *Portrait of the Artist as a Young Man*, tracing the amorous and psychological vicissitudes of an aspiring painter from his lonely childhood, through his troubled adolescence, up to his somewhat surprising marriage as a young adult.[4] Like Stephen Dedalus, Elmer's aesthetic and romantic development are intimately connected, yet Faulkner was concerned more with the growth of his protagonist's libido than Joyce had been, and, as critics have pointed out, his portrayal of Elmer's sexual maturation may also owe something to the writings of such diverse figures as Théophile Gautier and

Sigmund Freud.[5] Yet, despite the ambitiousness of the unfinished portrait, it seems that from the start Faulkner never
really had a firm grasp on his material and that, notwith-
standing the sanguine reports home, he remained unsure of
the treatment of his protagonist and genuinely uncertain
about what direction his story should take.

Elmer's psychosexual biography vacillates between em-
pathetic analysis and exaggerated burlesque; pathos and
comedy are often mingled to such an extent that it is impossible to ascertain the narrative intention. It is extremely
difficult, for example, to imagine how Faulkner was to rec-
oncile the ironic depiction of Elmer's wartime experience
with the sympathetic portrayal of his early childhood. Problems of tone and narrative distance are further complicated
by an increasingly elaborate plot and an ever-expanding cast
of characters. Book 3, with its detailed description of the
Monsons's transatlantic social climbing, moves the narrative progressively further away from Elmer and the concerns that had thus far seemed central.[6] And although this
satiric portrait of the decayed European nobility provides
some of the novel's liveliest comedy, it is clear, as Thomas
McHaney suggests, that "Elmer" was "doomed from the
moment the English aristocrats appear."[7]

Although "Elmer" failed as a novel, it contains a great
deal of material that Faulkner considered worth preserving
and, consistent with his former practice, he cannibalized the
abandoned text. He not only twice attempted to compress
the narrative into the form of a short story, but also reused
scenes, characters, and actual passages of text in a number
of subsequently published works. For example, Elmer's
Italian misadventure and incarceration (based on an actual
experience of Faulkner's traveling companion, William
Spratling)[8] provide the central incidents for the short story
"Divorce in Naples," while his romantic entanglement with
Ethel anticipates certain elements of Harry and Charlotte's

love affair in *The Wild Palms*.[9] Similar salvaging also supplied some of the dialogue and descriptions for the two novels that immediately followed "Elmer," and provided scenery and atmosphere for some of the short stories set in Europe. In *Mosquitoes*, for instance, large sections of Elmer's drunken fantasy are transferred en bloc and incorporated, without alteration, as a kind of symbolic gloss on the final chapter.[10] And for his characterization of Horace Benbow in *Flags in the Dust* Faulkner reused an entire two-page segment that had been originally employed to describe George Bleyth of "Elmer."[11] Although Elmer himself represents a type for which Faulkner had little subsequent use, other figures from the aborted novel also provide models for future characters. Elmer's beloved sister, Jo-Addie, clearly anticipates certain features of Caddy Compson and Addie Bundren,[12] whereas the epicene Myrtle Monson, whom Elmer envisions as a "Dianalike girl with an impregnable integrity, a slimness virginal and impervious to time,"[13] not only distinctly prefigures Patricia Robyn of *Mosquitoes* and the imagery usually associated with her, but also points backward to Cecily Saunders and a host of other elusive (and sometimes illusive) nymphs who appear in the contemporaneous poetry and short prose.

Other elements of "Elmer" also remained important for Faulkner and contributed substantively to his literary development. The novel's ambitious and innovative narrative technique, for example, demonstrates the young writer's undiminished involvement with formal experimentation and shows him once again directly confronting methods of presentation and organization that would aid in the formation of some of his later and more successful works. It seems very likely, as Cleanth Brooks argues, that the "general" structural model for "Elmer" was indeed Joyce's *A Portrait of the Artist as a Young Man* and, in particular, that Faulkner's focus on Elmer's sensitivity to colors and the private associations they hold for him was derived from the detailed portrayal of Stephen's fascination with language.[14] Just as Stephen's thoughts on the "beautiful word" wine set off a minimally connected group of ideas and recollections,[15] so Elmer's handling of the "virgin yet at the same time pregnant" tube of red paint triggers an elaborate series of personal memories.[16]

In "Elmer," however, it appears that Faulkner was attempting to take Joyce's strategy of psychologically resonant associations a step further. Despite frequent digressions and gaps, *Portrait of the Artist* moves steadily forward in time and is clearly designed to show the sequential stages of its protagonist's gradual maturation. Faulkner's text, on the other hand, begins with Elmer as an adult: he is aboard a ship bound for Europe, waiting to test the paints "in which was yet wombed his heart's desire."[17] The point where "Elmer" opens is, in fact, the very point where *Portrait of the Artist* ends, and though Elmer is not setting out specifically to "forge . . . the uncreated conscience of his race," he, like Stephen, is attempting to come to terms with a problematic artistic future. Thus, rather than work with what Joyce called "a fluid succession of presents"[18] and chart the various stages of Elmer's growth in the order of their occurrence, Faulkner begins in a more Conradian fashion with a critical moment of transition and, through an intricate series of flashbacks, dramatically shows its narrative significance.

These lengthy flashbacks, which make up most of the extant text, are keyed to Elmer's specific color associations; his personal aesthetic sensitivity, unlike Stephen's, thus plays a double role in the narrative, serving a structural as well as a thematic function. Elmer's fascination with the red tube of paint, for example, not only contributes specifically to his psychological portrait—symbolizing his obsessions and artistic aspirations—but also operates as a technical device, providing the means of making a smooth transition between events in his present and in his past. In this way, the fondled tube of pigment calls to Elmer's mind an important episode from his childhood, the "red horror" of the night his family's house burned. Perceptions of red also introduce the psychologically significant scene in which his sister leaves home, and it is not surprising that Elmer's memory of Jo-Addie is centered on the red crayon from the box that she subsequently sends him, and that he particularly refrains from damaging its "pointed symmetrical purity." The red-throated ventilators on the Captain's model ship prompt further recollections, and the same hue is explicitly associated with Elmer's first sexual encounter (remembered in terms of the girl's "full red mouth never quite completely closed") as well as with the crimson terror of his war service. Although Elmer eventually learns as an artist "that no color has any value, any significance save in its relation to other colors seen or suggested or imagined," the special associations that various colors hold for him constitute an important technical device, and other episodes in the novel are shaped by recollections connected with his perception of brown, green, or blue.[19]

Although there are several minor instances of flashback in *Soldiers' Pay* and the New Orleans prose, there is nothing in Faulkner's previous work that would prepare one for the boldly experimental temporal structure of "Elmer." Thomas McHaney suggests that the adoption of this structural design might have been directly influenced by Henri Bergson's concepts of time and memory,[20] but although there are certain general correspondences between Bergson's theories and the way in which Faulkner presents Elmer's consciousness, it may not be necessary to go beyond specifically literary works in a search for formal or conceptual models. Discontinuous time schemes and flashback techniques appear in much early twentieth-century fiction, and are especially prominent in the works of Conrad, Ford, and the

lesser literary impressionists, such as Beer and Hergesheimer, with whom Faulkner was familiar. The overall narrative strategy of "Elmer" can perhaps be best described as a
kind of innovative amalgam of Conrad and Joyce, where an
impressionistic handling of time is patterned on and keyed
to a solid framework of semantic or symbolic correspondences.[21] Though somewhat crude and exaggerated, this
technique is, on the whole, very effective, and it not only
points toward the elaborate flashback structures of such works
as *Light in August*, but also distinctly prefigures the general
formal methodology governing the first two sections of *The
Sound and the Fury*, where private associations control the
perception of time and shape the flow of narrative. Though
justifiably abandoned, "Elmer" shows Faulkner developing
his fictional craft by beginning an apprenticeship to new and
much more considerable literary "masters"—such as Joyce
and Conrad—and thereby discovering certain expressive
techniques and structural procedures that had to await a
more fully realized imaginative vehicle before they could
come to fruition.

At one point during the composition of "Elmer," Faulkner
put the novel aside, as he wrote his mother, in order to work
on "a sort of fairy tale" that had been "buzzing" in his head
(*L*, p. 22). Although there is no firm evidence to go on, it
seems very likely that this imaginative enterprise eventually
became *Mayday*, the forty-eight-page hand-lettered and il-
lustrated narrative, which Faulkner presented to Helen Baird
in the January following his European trip. Even though
this unique text has only recently been made generally available, *Mayday* has attracted some noteworthy critical attention. Although unwilling to accord it genuine literary merit,
Carvel Collins and Cleanth Brooks suggest that the "fairy
tale" constitutes an interesting—and in Collins's view, important—adjunct to the Faulkner canon, demonstrating certain obsessive themes and imagery as well as anticipating
elements of future works.[22]

Basically, *Mayday* is a pseudomedieval fantasy that relies on archaic diction and allegorical trappings in an attempt to present an ironic vision of disillusioned romantic love. Its protagonist, Sir Galwyn of Arthgyl, resembles the traditional knight-errant, and his adventures, though severely truncated, take the form of a quest narrative: accompanied by his squires, Pain and Hunger, he journeys through a magical wood in search of an ideal lover whose image he had glimpsed in a dream. Galwyn's brief and ultimately unsatisfying liaisons with Yseult, Elys, and Aelia trace the progress of this quest. And though all the women he encounters have special charms, none—not even the supernatural Aelia—even approaches his visionary ideal, who had appeared to him as "a face all young and red and white, and with long shining hair like a column of fair sunny water" calling to mind "young hyacinths in the spring, and honey and sunlight."[23] For Galwyn, earthly romance is all too transitory, and with each successive lover he becomes progressively more despondent. His quest ends on the banks of an enchanted river where he meets St. Francis and finds that his visionary lover is in fact "little sister Death" and that only by drowning himself can he attain her and remain true to his ideal.

Despite the portentousness of its underlying theme and its somber conclusion, *Mayday* is clearly designed as an ironic comedy and is very closely modeled on James Branch Cabell's *Jurgen*. Critics have drawn attention to the numerous similarities between *Mayday* and *Jurgen*, and the resemblances are so detailed in nature as to suggest that Faulkner was, once again, indulging in deliberate formal imitation. Following Michael Millgate's lead, Brooks and Collins have pointed out pervasive thematic, linguistic, structural, and stylistic correspondences between the two works.[24] And, to add to their list, it is worth noting that the typography, layout, and illustrations of *Mayday* are also derivative, distinctly reflecting the graphic design of the 1923 McBride

edition of *Jurgen*, which Faulkner gave to Stone that Christmas.[25]

Although *Mayday* is obviously based on *Jurgen*, Faulkner
was unable, or perhaps unwilling, to come close to dupli-
cating Cabell's wry tone, and there remain but the bare
bones of the joking anachronisms and cynical repartee that
characterized the original. For example, in an attempt to
follow Cabell's practice and undercut the allegorical mode
with humorously incongruous intrusions of "modern" common sense, Faulkner portrays father "Time" as a kind of
youthful Rotarian who offers Galwyn the following explanation for his atraditional personal appearance: "In this en-
lightened day when, as any standard magazine will inform
you, one's appearance depends purely on one's inclination
or disinclination to change it, what reason could I possibly
have for wishing to look older than I feel? Then my wife
(who, I am desolated to inform you, is away for the week-
end, visiting her parents) my wife thinks that it does not
look well for a man in my business to resemble a doddering
centenarian, particularly as my new system of doing business eliminates the middle man from all dealings with my
customers."[26] This passage, weak as it is, provides one of
the more successful instances of the work's attempt at verbal
humor. Some scenes, such as the description of Princess
Aelia's jealous tirade, are distinctly flatter, and the comedy
of *Mayday* appears for the most part almost amateurish when
compared to its model's.

Faulkner had an easier time with Cabell's pseudomedieval language and imagery, accommodating various
materials he had on hand to fit the tale's archaic context. In
this way, the symbolic tree from the rector's garden—which
played such a prominent role in *Soldiers' Pay*—becomes
transformed into an enchanted "tree covered with bright
never-still leaves of a thousand unimaginable colors"; on
speaking, it magically changes into "an old man with a long

shining beard like a silver cuirass" surrounded by "birds of a thousand kinds and colors."[27] Other elements from Faulkner's earlier work also found their way into *Mayday*. Princess Yseult's body, for example, is described in exactly the terms used to describe Cecily Saunders's—"a narrow pool of fair water"—while Sir Galwyn, like the "Wealthy Jew" in *The Double Dealer* sketch "New Orleans," is at one point depicted as "but a handful of damp clay." By the time *Mayday* was begun, St. Francis's mysterious "little sister Death" with "eyes the color of sleep" had already made an appearance in the *Times-Picayune* story "The Kid Learns" as well as in some of the unpublished verse. It also seems very likely that similar borrowing is responsible for the specific details surrounding Galwyn's watery rendezvous with her, since analogous imagery particularly associating drowning and transcendent love informs a number of Faulkner's early poems, including "Naiads' Song," as well as the early story "Nympholepsy."[28]

Critics, however, have been interested less in *Mayday*'s reflection of Faulkner's past than in its anticipation of his future. Brooks and Collins have especially noted the ways in which the depiction of Sir Galwyn's romantic disillusionment and suicide could have influenced Faulkner's description of Quentin Compson's final day in *The Sound and the Fury*, and Collins has further speculated that Galwyn's allegorical companions, Pain and Hunger, might have also in some way foreshadowed the use of Freudian structures that he sees underlying the basic design of *The Sound and the Fury*.[29] Despite, however, the demonstrable, if somewhat superficial, correspondences between Galwyn and Quentin, it seems dangerous to build too elaborate a theoretical framework on this highly derivative and fundamentally unsuccessful work. Although Faulkner devoted considerable time and energy to the work's physical appearance, the writing is sluggish and perfunctory, only occasionally equal to the quality of the New Orleans prose and certainly inferior to that of *Soldiers' Pay* and "Elmer." If, like the New Orleans exercises, it was undertaken as a deliberate study, Faulkner seems to have learned very little that could aid in his future development. When he is not serving stale Cabell, he is reheating leftover Faulkner, and, though intriguing for the critic, *Mayday* remains a very slight and extremely uneven production, pointing backward more often than forward.

While in Europe, Faulkner's creative activity, though very intense, was not especially profitable, and he returned home to Oxford for Christmas 1925 with few finished works and practically nothing ready for the printer.[30] Having abandoned two novels while on the continent, it seems likely enough, as his brother John suggests, that during the period immediately following this trip Faulkner would have concentrated on developing his talent for writing short stories.[31] There is, however, no firm evidence to indicate exactly what these works might have been. Because of their European subjects and settings, Faulkner's biographer, Joseph Blotner, has surmised that Faulkner may have drafted "Mistral," "Divorce in Naples," and "Victory" at this time, perhaps even before the publication of *Soldiers' Pay* on February 25, 1926, and its author's subsequent return to New Orleans. Even more tenuous biographical speculation is responsible for assigning "Black Music" and "Carcassonne" to this second New Orleans sojourn, and Blotner so dates them solely because he perceives that these works may have been influenced by Sherwood Anderson's descriptions of the Virginia farm where he had stayed while Faulkner was in Europe.[32] Yet, even assuming that Blotner's dates of composition are roughly accurate, there is no evidence to show that any of these stories, with the exception of "Mistral," ever reached a publishable form before 1930.[33] The quality of writing in "Carcassonne," to take the most extreme example, definitely suggests Faulkner's more mature style and, indeed, it seems quite unlikely that this highly effective, if fundamentally ambiguous, evocation of imaginative transcendence could have followed so closely on "The Artist" section of *The Double Dealer* sketch and the allegorical fantasy of "Elmer," which are vastly inferior attempts to deal with the same basic theme. Although it is very difficult to determine exactly what Faulkner wrote during the period following his return from Europe, the second New Orleans stay was not nearly as fruitful, imaginatively or educationally, as his earlier visit.[34] Despite the favorable reviews *Soldiers' Pay* was receiving at this time, Faulkner must have been acutely conscious that even though he had been actively engaged in his craft all the while, he had not completed anything publishable since he had submitted that first novel the previous summer.

Faulkner's literary ambition, however, remained strong, and in June 1926, shortly after the New Orleans visit, he took up temporary residence at Pascagoula on the Mississippi gulf coast, where he immediately began another extended work of prose fiction. Despite, or perhaps because of, the recent period of relative unproductivity, commercial as well as aesthetic, this novel, entitled *Mosquitoes*, appears to have progressed smoothly. With the evidence currently available, it is impossible to determine what relation Faulkner's new work of fiction bears to "Mosquito," the novel that he had begun in Europe. If, however, he was reworking some form of that text he seems to have encountered none of the problems that caused him to abandon his first attempt, since the Pascagoula typescript was finished on September 1, just about three months after it was begun.[35] Although it is possible that Faulkner had simply learned "enough about people" in the intervening year to complete the project as originally conceived (*L*, p. 14), the relative ease with which he drafted *Mosquitoes* seems to be due more to his reliance on an essentially derivative narrative strategy and existing materials than to any real advance in outlook, philosophical perspective, or fictional technique. The finished novel, as practically every critic has noted, is closely patterned on the then fashionable "novel of ideas" and is particularly indebted to the extremely popular early works of Aldous Huxley, the founder and most notable exponent of the genre. The commercial success of this kind of fiction may have significantly contributed to Faulkner's conception of *Mosquitoes*, and he quite possibly had an eye toward financial prospects when he began what he himself later called this "trashily smart" novel (*L*, p. 40). His letter to Anita Loos, written only a few months before *Mosquitoes*, is frankly envious of the success of her recent best-seller, *Gentlemen Prefer Blondes* (*L*, p. 32).

There has been much discussion of the relationship between *Mosquitoes* and Huxley's works, and although there are undoubtedly parallels between Faulkner's second novel and *Crome Yellow* (1921), Huxley's later book, *Those Barren Leaves* (1925), seems a much more likely model.[36] First of all, the plot (the pattern of persistent inaction) of both novels is roughly the same: an aging, self-styled patroness of the arts gives a party for a heterogeneous group of people, mostly artists, in an isolated setting, allowing the guests enough leisure for a great deal of talk and for various attempts at amorous involvement. This basic situation is common enough in the literature of the period, appearing, for example, in such popular works as Norman Douglas's *South Wind* (with which, incidentally, *Mosquitoes* was initially compared) and by itself provides little evidence of Faulkner's direct familiarity with Huxley's text.[37] The characterizations of the hostesses in the two novels, however, exhibit much closer correspondences: Mrs. Aldwinkle of *Those Barren Leaves*, like Faulkner's Mrs. Maurier, is no longer married and appears eminently available. Both women, moreover, have rebellious young nieces and spend their time entertaining unappreciative artists at their own expense. The most striking feature of their resemblance, however, lies in their aesthetic attitudes, which they express in very similar terms. On entering into an artistic discussion, Mrs. Maurier characteristically explains, "You . . . know how sensitive to beauty I am, though I have been denied the creative impulse myself" (*M*, p. 23), while Mrs. Aldwinkle declares, "I'm one of those unfortunate people . . . who have an artistic temperament without an artist's powers."[38]

Resemblances, of varying degrees, have also been noted between other characters from the two novels: between the erudite and critical Mr. Cardon of *Those Barren Leaves* and Julius, "the Semitic man," of *Mosquitoes*;[39] between Huxley's poet Francis Chelifer and Faulkner's "ghostly" versifier, Mark Frost; between the female artists, Mary Thirlow—the novelist from *Those Barren Leaves*—and Dorothy Jameson, the "humorless" painter from *Mosquitoes*; and finally, between the two nonintellectual and unartistic couples, Huxley's Miss Elver and her brother, and Jenny and Pete in *Mosquitoes*.[40] Similar incidents of amorous byplay also mark affinities between the two works, and the characters in *Mosquitoes*, like those in *Those Barren Leaves*, frequently discuss the problems of artistic representation, the futility of communication, and the uncertainty of romantic love.

The presence of Huxley, and especially of *Those Barren Leaves*, in *Mosquitoes* is, however, more pervasive than a mere list of character correspondences or thematic parallels could indicate. As we have seen, the persistent literary borrowing that characterizes almost all of Faulkner's apprentice work involves techniques, styles, and structural methods as often as character types, themes, or elements of plot. In a University of Virginia class conference of 1957, Faulkner, speaking of Thomas Beer, indicated the kinds of things he appropriated during this period: "I got quite a lot from him—

[he] was to me a good tool, a good method, a good usage of words, approach to incident" (*FU*, p. 20). In practically all of his early works, and especially in his two preceding projects, "Elmer" and *Mayday*, Faulkner had drawn heavily on literary models available to him from his reading in an attempt to understand "à fond," as Wright had put it, "the principles of his predecessors" and to assimilate directly the received conventions of his chosen discipline.[41] By the time he came to write *Mosquitoes*, he had already provided himself with many "good tools" as a result of exploring a wide range of styles and techniques, including the narrative strategy of Aldous Huxley's "novel of ideas."

In his early novels, Huxley presents the disparity between ideas and action principally by means of two related, yet ultimately distinct, fictional techniques. The omniscient narrator of *Crome Yellow*, for example, frequently calls attention to the inadequacy or implausibility of a certain character's observations by contrasting interior views with narratively authoritative commentary—an ironic strategy employed by Faulkner throughout *Soldiers' Pay* to portray Lowe's anachronistic romanticism, Cecily's persistent superficiality, and George Farr's seemingly hopeless sexual attachment. Yet Huxley's works also exhibit a more flexible and sophisticated narrative technique that Faulkner uses only minimally, and with limited effectiveness, in his first novel. In *Those Barren Leaves*, and to a lesser degree in *Crome Yellow*, Huxley presents various ideas in conflict, in the heat of inception, through endless conversations among a group of highly articulate characters. "The character of each personage," Huxley would later state, "must be implied, as far as possible, in the ideas of which he is the mouth-piece. In so far as theories are rationalizations of sentiments, instincts, dispositions of soul, this is feasible."[42] As his novels unfold, the conversations become progressively more revelatory; personal theories are modified and cherished concepts undergo the scrutiny of other intelligences. This play of ideas allows the expression of a great range of opinions and speculative theories, which are subsequently tested, usually with ironic results, in further discussions and in dramatic confrontations.

Faulkner had first explored a rather crude version of this technique in chapter 2 of *Soldiers' Pay*, where the rector and Januarius Jones—strangers up to this point—immediately join in a lengthy intellectual discussion which remains almost totally unrelated to the novel's central concerns (*SP*, pp. 58–64). In *Mosquitoes*, the conversations, which make up a large proportion of the text, follow Huxley's models more closely and operate on just the same pattern as those in *Those Barren Leaves*. They unsystematically examine the novel's dominant themes—in this case, sex, language, and art—as well as numerous other topics, and present a network of ideas which are progressively interrelated, redefined, and tested as the action unfolds and further discussions are introduced. A typical dialogue between Dawson Fairchild, a novelist modeled on Sherwood Anderson, and Julius (commonly called "the Semitic man"), a highly educated and cynical critic, is initiated by an observation concerning their companion Talliaferro's repeated and unsuccessful attempts at sexual seduction:

> "Now, there goes the Great Illusion, par excellence."
> "What's Talliaferro's trouble?" asked the Semitic man.
> "The illusion that you can seduce women. Which you can't. They just elect you."
> "And then, Gold [*sic*] help you," the other added.
> "And with words, at that," Fairchild continued. "With words," he repeated savagely.
> "Well, why not with words? One thing gets along with women as well as another. And you are a funny sort to disparage words; you, a member of that species all of whose actions are controlled by words. It's the word that overturns

thrones and political parties and instigates vice crusades, not
things: the Thing is merely the symbol for the Word. And
more than that, think what a devil of a fix you and I'd be in
were it not for words, were we to lose our faith in words. I'd
have nothing to do all day long, and you'd have to work or
starve to death. . . . And, after all, his illusion is just as
nourishing as yours. Or mine, either."

"I know: but yours or mine ain't quite so ridiculous as
his is."

"How do you know they aren't?" Fairchild had no reply,
and the other continued: "After all, it doesn't make any
difference what you believe. Man is not only nourished by
convictions, he is nourished by any conviction. . . . So don't
you go around feeling superior to Talliaferro. I think his
present illusion and its object are rather charming, almost as
charming as the consummation of it would be—which is more
than you can say for yours. . . . And so do you, you poor
emotional eunuch; so do you, despite that bastard of a surgeon
and a stenographer which you call your soul, so do you
remember with regret kissing in the dark and all the tender
and sweet stupidity of young flesh." [*M*, pp. 130–31]

Unlike the rector-Jones dialogue from *Soldiers' Pay*, this
colloquy has no underlying ironic substructure; the emphasis falls on the topic under discussion rather than on the
dramatic interplay between the characters, and the ideas
presented specifically reflect some of the novel's central
concerns and thus significantly contribute to the ever-
developing web of narrative relationships between sexual
behavior, artistic expression, linguistic competence, and
personal integration.

Consistent with Huxley's "novel of ideas" strategy, Julius's opinions on language, sex, art, and age are re-
evaluated in other dialogues, as well as in patterns of dramatic
incident, and a framework of ethical response gradually
emerges. Thus the "illusion," as Julius puts it, "that words
control actions" is not only explicitly satirized in Talliafer-

ro's consistently unsuccessful search for the one conversational gambit—the theoretical "trick"—that will make him
irresistible to women, but it is also dramatized through the
barrenness and irrelevance of the myriad shipboard discussions themselves: "Talk, talk, talk: the utter and heartbreak-
ing stupidity of words. It seemed endless, as though it might
go on forever. Ideas, thoughts, became mere sounds to be
bandied about until they were dead" (*M*, p. 186).[43] As the
novel progresses, other major themes are introduced, and,
like Julius's speculations on language, they function as evaluative instruments against which individual characters and
relationships between characters can be judged. This persistent pattern of narrative assessment makes the "novel of
ideas" a perfect vehicle for satire, and *Mosquitoes*, like
Those Barren Leaves, sharply ridicules the foibles and pre-
tenses of most of its characters.

The "novel of ideas," as almost all of Huxley's early
works demonstrate, is an inherently flexible genre, which is
able to accommodate a great variety of diverse, and sometimes disparate, materials. In *Those Barren Leaves*, for instance, Huxley frequently offers the reader examples of his
characters' heterogeneous literary productions, and the text
contains numerous poems, sections of a novel, a draft short
story, and, most notably, extended "Fragments from the
Autobiography of Francis Chelifer." Faulkner includes similar literary interpolations in *Mosquitoes*. There are not only
Fairchild's coherently structured reminiscences of his col-
lege days (*M*, pp. 115–20), his anecdote concerning the
"romance" in the "privy" (*M*, pp. 231–34),[44] and his splendid Al Jackson tall tales (*M*, pp. 66–68, 86–88, 277–78),
but there are also sections of Eva Wiseman's *Satyricon in
Starlight*, or, as Major Ayers calls it, "the syphilis poem"
(*M*, pp. 247, 249, 252), including the complete sonnet
"Hermaphroditus," discussed in chapter 1 above. Almost all
of this literary material, needless to say, derives from Faulk-

ner's creative past: given the extent to which he reused elements from his earlier work in *Soldiers' Pay* and *Mayday*—successfully and unsuccessfully—it is hardly surprising that the structurally more adaptable *Mosquitoes* should contain similar self-borrowing.

What is, however, surprising is the quantity and frequency of this practice and the degree to which Faulkner used *Mosquitoes* to accommodate the miscellaneous materials he had on hand. Some of the borrowing, like that in *Soldiers' Pay* and *Mayday*, consists of refurbished descriptive passages or favorite phrases, such as the description of "Andrew Jackson in childish effigy bestriding the terrific arrested plunge of his curly balanced horse" (*M*, p. 14), which first appeared in the *Times-Picayune* story, "Out of Nazareth" (*NO*, p. 46); or David West's epiphanylike memory of "riding a freight into San Francisco" (*M*, p. 162), which is clearly based on the "Frankie and Johnny" section of "New Orleans" (*NO*, p. 6); or Julius's paraphrase of the quotation in "Wealthy Jew" from *Mademoiselle de Maupin*: "I love three things: gold, marble and purple . . . form solidity color" (*M*, p. 340). Other borrowings, especially those based on unpublished works, involve a more extensive use of existing texts. The Al Jackson tales, of course, closely follow the letters Faulkner had written in collaboration with Sherwood Anderson the preceding year, and the fragments from *Satyricon in Starlight* echo segments of poems he had drafted during his stay in Europe.[45]

Unpublished materials also provide the setting and incidents for portions of the text offered as having been composed by the fictional characters. And though it is impossible to ascertain the influence of the abandoned "Mosquito," the entire closing episode dealing with Talliaferro's final and devastatingly unsuccessful attempt to seduce Jenny once existed separately as a short story entitled "Don Giovanni."[46] The surrealistic fantasy, interspersed in italics throughout the final chapter (*M*, pp. 335–40), is perhaps the most notable product of Faulkner's literary salvaging. As already indicated, this rhetorically self-indulgent vision (whose obscure images of oriental pageantry, incidentally, owe much to Flaubert's *La Tentation de Saint Antoine*)[47] originally appeared in a longer form in "Elmer," where one might attempt to justify its inclusion in the narrative by positing a symbolic interpretation—arguing, for example, that the two lavishly described female figures might signify Elmer's twin romantic entanglements, and the shadowy beggar grasping a crust might represent the protagonist's nebulous artistic aspirations. In any case, the "*young naked boy daubed with vermilion, carrying casually a crown*" (*M*, p. 337)—who appears in both versions[48]—symbolizes the youthful Elmer and specifically reflects his characteristic predilection for red.

When incorporating this material into the final chapter of *Mosquitoes*, Faulkner merely removed some of the more outlandish figures from the Dionysiac procession ("an elephant like a snow-bank," "six torchbearers bearing torches," "a girl with straight hair neither brown nor gold,")[49] and added a new image denoting Gordon's marble statue, which had been previously associated with the sculptor's romantic idealization of Patricia Robyn: "*the headless, armless, legless torso of a girl, motionless and virginal and passionately eternal*" (*M*, p. 339). This apotheosis of Gordon's "feminine ideal"—as he once called the statue—is juxtaposed to Julius and Fairchild's drunken discussions on artistic creativity and imaginative transcendence, and the italicized passage closely precedes Fairchild's often-quoted definition of genius: "that Passion Week of the heart, that instant of timeless beatitude . . . in which the hackneyed accidents which make up this world . . . brought together by chance in perfect proportions, take on a kind of splendid and timeless beauty" (*M*, p. 339). The proximity of these two passages, along with the climactic position of the whole *Walpurgisnacht* episode, has caused some critics to see the entire italicized fantasy as a kind of emblematic affirmation of Gordon's artistic mission.[50] Still, it remains difficult to perceive any relationship between the series of strange symbolic figures appropriated, without alteration, from "Elmer"—the beggar, the priests, the women in golden chains, and especially the vermilion boy—and the *"headless, armless, legless torso of a girl,"* the only image specifically associated with Gordon and his art.

This dream vision—like the other interpolated narrative, the italicized Arabian tale concerning *"Halim"* and the illusive *"maid"* (*M*, pp. 269–73)—is never fully integrated into the text, and it remains only minimally connected to the novel's central concerns. Although it is possible, as critics have suggested, that this material offers a kind of abstract parable of the sculptor's aesthetic credo, it seems much more likely that it represents yet another example of Faulkner's stylistic exploration—another opportunity to indulge in the romantic excesses of "Elmer." Whatever the motivation, however, the flexible "novel of ideas" framework allowed Faulkner to incorporate the italicized fantasy with little consideration for contextual relevance, and taken as a whole, as Michael Millgate points out, *Mosquitoes* remains "a kind of rag-bag into which [Faulkner] could gather up all the usable odds-and-ends of his brief literary past."[51]

The "rag-bag" also contains considerable evidence of Faulkner's reading and, along with the pervasive influence of Huxley, critics have tracked down a number of the novel's more conspicuous literary debts. Some of the derivative passages in *Mosquitoes*, quite unlike the majority of Faulkner's apprentice borrowings, are deliberately allusive and satiric in intent. It has been pointed out, for example, that the echoes from Conrad's "Heart of Darkness" which are woven throughout Faulkner's description of the swampy north shore of Lake Pontchartrain set up general correspondences between the two texts which are then ironically undercut as contrasting details emerge.[52] Other obviously derivative passages may have been similarly motivated; yet it is extremely difficult, for instance, to see any purpose, ironic or otherwise, for the concentrated amalgam of Lafcadio Hearn, Joyce, Eliot, and perhaps Omar Khayyám that appears in the novel's prologue: "Outside the window New Orleans, the vieux carré, brooded in a faintly tarnished languor like an aging yet still beautiful courtesan in a smoke-filled room, avid yet weary too of ardent ways. Above the city summer was hushed warmly into the bowled weary passion of the sky. Spring and the cruellest months were gone, the cruel months, the wantons that break the fat hybernatant dullness and comfort of Time; August was on the wing, and September—a month of languorous days regretful as woodsmoke" (*M*, pp. 10–11). The description of the Vieux Carré as a jaded courtesan echoes Lafcadio Hearn's "The Glamour of New Orleans" (as well as Faulkner's "New Orleans"),[53] while the phrase "weary too of ardent ways" represents a slight variation on the first line of the villanelle from *A Portrait of the Artist*. "Spring and the cruellest months," of course, alludes to the opening of Eliot's *The Waste Land*, and Faulkner's peculiar usage of "bowled," as Brooks suggests, seems to have been derived from either the *Rubáiyát* or *Ulysses*.[54]

Although there are only a few instances of such density of allusion in *Mosquitoes*, there is ample evidence of more covert borrowing, and critics have not hesitated to point out Faulkner's debts to Joyce, Eliot, Hergesheimer, and even Rostand.[55] More critical energy, however, has been expended in discussing the ways in which specific conversations in *Mosquitoes* reflect Faulkner's aesthetic concerns at this stage of his development. Aside from basic questions of creative inspiration and the role of the artist in society,

there are frequent dialogues on such pertinent topics as fictional mimesis, geographical determinism, and, perhaps most
significantly, the limits of regionalism. Yet it seems very
risky to read too much of Faulkner into these speculative
exchanges, especially since a good number of the ideas
presented—particularly the notions of regionalism—may
have been derived from Wright and designed to advance
general rather than personal positions,[56] whereas other ideas
seem determined more by considerations of characterization
and verisimilitude than by any encompassing analytical inquiry.

Mosquitoes, as almost every commentator has noted, is
in part a roman à clef, and, very possibly, certain abstract
positions taken by the individual characters are designed
chiefly to reflect the actual speech and ideas of a real-life
prototype. It is generally agreed, for example, that Julius,
"the Semitic man," is closely modeled on Julius Weis Friend,
one of the editors of *The Double Dealer*, and an examination of Friend's editorial contributions indicates the extent
to which the fictional figure's intellectual concerns and literary opinions reflect those of the original subject.[57] Julius's
critical assessment of his friend Dawson Fairchild's artistic
limitations, for instance, seems consistent with the tenor of
Friend's literary judgments, and it is possible that Faulkner
might have actually heard Friend express similar sentiments
concerning their common friend Sherwood Anderson.[58]

Many of Dawson Fairchild's literary pronouncements seem
to be similarly motivated, and though the predominantly
satiric portrayal of a sincere but fumbling novelist might
subconsciously indicate "a gesture of irreverence toward a
literary father figure"[59] or an attempt to "shake off Anderson's influence,"[60] there is much in Fairchild's speech that
accurately and positively reflects Anderson's language and
thought. A number of Fairchild's views are very closely
related to ideas expressed in Anderson's published works.

On the basic disparity between reality and fiction, for example, Fairchild states: "In life, anything might happen; in actual life people will do anything. It's only in books that people must function according to arbitrary rules of conduct and probability; it's only in books that events must never flout credulity" (*M*, p. 181). Anderson had written: "Anything may happen in life. We all know that. People hardly ever do as as [*sic*] we think they should. There are no plot short stories in life."[61] People, he asserted, "do not converse in the book world as they do in life. Scenes of the imaginative world are not real scenes. . . . The life of reality is confused, disorderly, almost always without apparent purpose, whereas in the artist's imaginative life there is purpose."[62]

The fictional novelist's opinions on the potentialities of language as an aesthetic medium also reflect Anderson's views, and although, at one point, Fairchild, like Julius, notes the tendency for verbalization to move away from experience toward empty abstractions ("it is a kind of sterility—words"), he just as strongly maintains a firm belief in the creative power of language: "I don't claim that words have life in themselves. But words brought into a happy conjunction produce something that lives, just as soil and climate and an acorn in proper conjunction will produce a tree" (*M*, p. 210). Anderson had expressed a very similar position: "I have not lost my faith in words. . . . There is no reason at all why I should not have been able, by the instrumentality of these little words, why I should not have been able to give you the very smell of the little street wherein I have just walked."[63] Yet Anderson was equally aware of the barrenness of the mere proliferation of words and, like Fairchild and Julius, was especially cognizant of the limitations of aesthetic discussion. In *Winesburg, Ohio*, for example, his portrait of the "talking artists" can be seen to have particular relevance for the characters of *Mosqui-*

toes: "Every-one knows of the talking artists. Throughout all of the known history of the world they have gathered in rooms and talked. They talk of art and are passionately, almost feverishly, in earnest about it. They think it matters much more than it does. . . . Words were said about line and values and composition, lots of words, such as are always being said."[64]

Although there is no direct evidence of Anderson's reaction to his characterization as Dawson Fairchild, the converse situation—Anderson's use of Faulkner as the model for his protagonist in "A Meeting South," which appeared in *The Dial* for April 1925—seems to have greatly affected the younger writer, and in a 1955 interview he retrospectively described Anderson's artistic decline specifically in terms of this fictional gambit: "I think when a writer reaches the point when he's got to write about people he knows, his friends, then he has reached the tragic point. There seems to me there's too much to be written about . . . for one to have to resort to actual living figures" (*LG*, p. 120). This criticism, of course, could be easily applied to *Mosquitoes* itself, Faulkner's own and more extended roman à clef. And although it is unfair to present his assessment of Anderson's failure as if it were a tacit acknowledgment of his own imaginative lapse, his portrayal of the creative weakness implicit in adopting a roman à clef strategy—the use of "actual living figures" only as a last resort—seems relevant, especially since so much of *Mosquitoes* depends on the use of other kinds of models.

Faulkner once admitted that he thought *Mosquitoes* was a "bad book" (*LG*, p. 92), one, in retrospect, that he "probably wouldn't write . . . at all" (*FU*, p. 257). However, he also made it clear that he was "not ashamed of it," because it "was the chips, the badly sawn planks that the carpenter produces while he's learning to be a first-rate carpenter" (*FU*, p. 257). The novel's derivative, "rag-bag" character, its excessive reliance on prototypes and existing texts, corroborates Faulkner's judgment and indicates the degree to which *Mosquitoes* remains the kind of apprentice work he would have to leave behind. Far more than in *Soldiers' Pay*, or even in the more polished sections of "Elmer," appropriated materials remain unassimilated, disparate episodes seem almost randomly juxtaposed, and the text's jagged edges and rough seams frequently obtrude. It is extremely difficult, for example, to determine the thematic or structural relevance of the extended interlude in the swamp, the description of Major Ayers's financial schemes, or the detailed depiction of Pete Ginotta's family business. Following the failure of "Elmer" and the extended period of relative unproductivity (creative and financial) which preceded his trip to Pascagoula, Faulkner must have felt a certain pressure to publish; *Mosquitoes* seems to be the result of that pressure. Though he had discovered his prodigious technical abilities by the time he came to write this second novel, he had yet to find his proper narrative materials, and *Mosquitoes*'s fundamentally derivative design, slapdash composition, nonfunctional formal heterogeneity, and over-reliance on self-borrowing indicate the inhibiting desperateness of his search.

Like the more successful apprentice works, however, *Mosquitoes* is exploratory as well as imitative. Its inherently elastic narrative format, indeed, provided Faulkner with an excellent opportunity to continue his technical experimentation and to try out various stylistic and structural devices. Some of these experiments, such as the interpolated narratives, are more important for what they attempted than for what they accomplished. Others show a genuine achievement and point, however hesitantly, toward Faulkner's future work. The interior monologues in *Mosquitoes*, for example, mark a definite advance over those in *Soldiers' Pay* and show Faulkner moving away from traditional *er-*

lebte Rede toward less restrictive methods of portraying the modulations of consciousness. Certain passages, most notably those describing David West's feverish hallucinations as he attempts to carry Patricia through the mosquito-ridden swamp, rely on the detailed depiction of the nuances and rhythms of the subject's inner voice: "Two steps more. No, three steps now. Three steps. Getting to be afternoon, getting to be later than it was once. Three steps, then. All right. Man walks on his hind legs; a man can take three steps, a monkey can take three steps, but there is water in a monkey's cage, in a pan. Three steps. All right. One. Two. Three. Gone. Gone. Gone. It's a red sound. Not behind your eyes. Sea. See. Sea. See. You're in a cave, you're in a cave of dark sound, the sound of the sea is outside the cave. Sea. See. See. See" (*M*, p. 206).

Other interior views more closely resemble the stream of consciousness techniques introduced by Joyce and Woolf. These passages are characterized by the unpunctuated juxtaposition of fragmentary thoughts, phrases, ideas, and images, and they are designed to create the illusion of an unmediated presentation of ongoing mental activity. Faulkner employs this strategy to articulate Gordon's inner tensions and to emphasize, through contrasting poetical images and literary allusions, the conflict between his will and desire:

> what would i say to her fool fool you have work to do you have nothing accursed intolerant and unclean too warm your damn bones then whisky will do as well or a chisel and maul any damn squirrel keeps warm in a cage go on go on then israfel revolted surprised behind a haycock by a male relation fortitude become a matchflame snuffed by a small white belly where was it i once saw a dogwood tree not white but tan tan as cream what will you say to her bitter and new as a sunburned flame bitter and new those two little silken snails somewhere under her dress horned pinkly yet reluctant o

israfel ay wax your wings with the thin odorless moisture of
her thighs strangle your heart with hair fool fool cursed and
forgotten of god [*M*, p. 48]

Although in *Mosquitoes* itself these techniques remain frequently awkward and oblique, they represent early versions
of some of Faulkner's most sophisticated formal experiments and anticipate central features of the radically innovative interior monologues of *The Sound and the Fury*.

Other devices from *Mosquitoes* contributed materials and
methods for Faulkner's future development. Julius's encap-
sulated biography of Mrs. Maurier (*M*, pp. 323–26), for
instance, shows Faulkner effectively exploring Conradian
techniques of conjectural narration,[65] a fictional mode that
informs a number of his future works—most notably *Absalom, Absalom!*—and that, in the later stages of his career,
becomes quite a characteristic expressive strategy. Julius's
imaginative reconstruction is based partly on secondhand
information (details passed on from his grandfather), partly
on his awareness of literary conventions and his sense of
formal harmony. Like Shreve and Quentin's much more
elaborate narrative speculations, Julius's tale relies on hy-
pothetical formulations, and his description of Mrs. Maurier's wedding ceremony, for example, is replete with
evocations of what necessarily "would have" happened, of
what "must have" occurred, in order to conform with some
underlying notion of aesthetic or psychological appropri-
ateness.

Some formal experiments in *Mosquitoes* depend on the
text's overriding pattern of intersecting conversation and
debate. As the novel progresses, Faulkner supplements the
numerous intellectual exchanges with more adventurous
evocations of verbal intercourse and employs narrative
strategies that bring the dialectical voices to the fore. As in
Soldiers' Pay, he occasionally breaks the text into a playlike

format (for example, *M*, pp. 237–39) and, at one point, even eschews labeling the speakers altogether, so that the voices stand by themselves:

> Come on, Mark, you've got to go. All the men will be needed, hey, Mrs. Maurier?
> Yes, indeed; indeed, yes. All the men must help.
> Sure: all you brave strong men have got to go.
> I'm a poet, not an oarsman. I can't—
> So is Eva: look at her, she's going.
> Shelley could row a boat.
> Yes, and remember what happened to him, too. [*M*, p. 193]

Mosquitoes, in fact, goes a long way in the direction of the novel as play, as pure dialogue.[66] The speculative discussions, along with the many other forms of verbal exchange, distinctly point toward such dramatic structures as *Requiem for a Nun*, as well as toward the larger dialectical strategies that underlie such works as *Go Down, Moses*, *The Town*, and even *Absalom, Absalom!* At the time he wrote *Mosquitoes*, however, Faulkner had yet to learn that such dialogues only become dramatic if they are clearly and consistently revelatory of character, and in the intellectual debates there is not a sufficient sense of the principal speakers' personalities for the reader to be able to keep them clearly apart as they talk.

Although somewhat ad hoc in conception and certainly imitative in structure and execution, *Mosquitoes* provided Faulkner with an opportunity to experiment with—and finally get out of his creative system—a whole range of contemporary styles and influences. Just as his writing about New Orleans reflected a stage in his career that he was about to leave behind, so his indulgence in an extravagant variety of literary styles and narrative strategies can be seen retrospectively as an indication that he would indulge in them no more, that they were somehow more appropriate to the pseudoartists with whom the novel chiefly dealt. If studying Huxley, Cabell, and Hergesheimer could only take him so far, further preparation was still required before he could take advantage of such formidable "masters" as Conrad and Joyce. Although on the whole a "bad book," as Faulkner rightly judged, *Mosquitoes* is, as Conrad Aiken noted in his review, "good enough to make one wish that it were better."[67] Faulkner wrote it in the last stages of his apprenticeship, when he wrote "for the sake of writing because it was fun," before he found out that "the whole output or sum of an artist's work had to have a design" (*LG*, p. 255), and, more significantly, before he had fully discovered what materials (his or others', past or present) could contribute to that design.

5.
Expedition into Regionalism
"Father Abraham" and
Flags in the Dust

In late 1926 and early 1927, while Liveright was busy deleting from *Mosquitoes* a number of its more prurient passages, Faulkner had begun drafting two distinct yet related works of fiction which had very little in common with the "smart" novel that was undergoing the editorial process. Despite various auxiliary projects, he had completed enough of the new novels by the winter for his friend Phil Stone to write an enthusiastic press notice: "Both are Southern in setting. One is something of a saga of an extensive family connection of typical 'poor white trash' and is said by those who have seen that part of the manuscript completed to be the funniest book anybody ever wrote. The other is a tale of the aristocratic, chivalrous and ill-fated Sartoris family, one of whom was even too reckless for the daring Confederate cavalry leader, Jeb Stuart. Both are laid in Mississippi."[1]

The comic "saga" that Stone describes undoubtedly corresponds to—or at least included—"Father Abraham," the incomplete and still unpublished manuscript that first de-

lineates the social and economic environment of Frenchman's Bend, introduces the acquisitive and unscrupulous
Snopeses ("a race that is of the land and yet rootless"),
relates the story of the unmanageable Texas ponies, and
contains, in short, much of the material that would eventually appear in *The Hamlet* and in various stories over the
next thirty years.[2] Faulkner's other project, the "tale" of the
established Sartoris family, was of course *Flags in the Dust*,
the original uncut version of the novel (first published in
1973) that was to be substantially revised and published as
Sartoris in 1929. Although overly optimistic about the
achievement of "Father Abraham," Stone's brief announce-
ment accurately isolates what is perhaps the most significant
feature of these texts, the one that links them together and
distinguishes them from all of Faulkner's previous productions: "Both works are Southern in setting. . . . Both works
are laid in Mississippi." Both works, more specifically and
importantly, deal with Yocona—the original name for "Yoknapatawpha"—County, a densely imagined province modeled closely on the north Mississippi region where Faulkner
lived, and in writing them he discovered and first adum-
brated the geographical, historical, cultural, and social lin-
eaments of what was to become his self-contained fictional
domain.

It was fitting that Stone should herald Faulkner's initial
foray into his indigenous locale. Stone was more actively
involved with the inception of "Father Abraham" and *Flags
in the Dust* than with any of Faulkner's other fiction: Faulkner dedicated the Snopes Trilogy to "Phil Stone—who did
half the laughing for thirty years," and Stone stated that he
had "invented more of *Sartoris* than . . . any of the other
books."[3] More significantly, it was Stone who had stressed
Faulkner's provincial roots from the very beginning of his
literary career, before his writing showed even the slightest
indication of a regional perspective. In the preface to *The*

Marble Faun, Stone had forcibly emphasized Faulkner's profound sense of place: "The author of these poems is a man steeped in the soil of his native land, a Southerner by every instinct, and, more than that, a Mississippian. George Moore said that all universal art became great by first being provincial, and the sunlight and mocking-birds and blue hills of North Mississippi are a part of this young man's very being" (*MF*, p. 7). If at this time Faulkner was as deeply immersed in the local landscape as Stone suggests, very little of this experience found its way into his verse; as critics have shown, the flora and fauna of *The Marble Faun* derive more from literary prototypes than from any sustained attempt to render the "blue hills" of north Mississippi.[4]

Stone's exaggerated assessment of Faulkner's use of his native terrain was decidedly premature. Faulkner's contemporaneous literary essays, however, reveal an attitude toward regionalism strikingly similar to Stone's and even (in one instance) anticipatory of it. As early as 1922, Faulkner wrote that "art is preeminently provincial: i.e., it comes directly from a certain age and a certain locality" (*EP*, p. 86); and in the 1924 essay "Verse Old and Nascent: A Pilgrimage,"[5] he praised A. E. Housman specifically for evoking "the beauty of being of the soil like a tree" and added that he had himself "fixed" his "roots" in his native "soil" (*EP*, pp. 116–17). Similar, though more problematical, discussions concerning the geographical specificity of literature inform a number of the abstract exchanges in *Mosquitoes*, and throughout his apprenticeship Faulkner was at least intellectually aware of the expressive possibilities inherent in a regional perspective. Until he began "Father Abraham" and *Flags in the Dust*, however, he did little more than pay lip service to an imaginative involvement with north Mississippi, and apart from "Mississippi Hills: My Epitaph,"[6] certain passages in "The Liar," "The Hill," and "Nympholepsy," and a scene or two in *Soldiers' Pay*,[7] indigenous material is virtually absent from the work produced during this apprentice period. Years later, in 1948, Faulkner told Malcolm Cowley that he had "commenced with the idea that novels should deal with imaginary scenes and people— so *Soldiers' Pay* was laid in Georgia, where he had never been."[8] Similar thinking was probably responsible for locating the American sections of "Elmer" in Arkansas and Texas; and though *Mosquitoes* certainly does not depict wholly "imaginary scenes and people," its fictional setting has little connection with Faulkner's native environment.

Although Phil Stone, or *The Creative Will*, may have provided some of the impetus, Faulkner suggested in a late essay that it was Sherwood Anderson who first advised him to mine his local terrain, insisting that "you have to have somewhere to start from: then you begin to learn. . . . It dont matter where it was, just so you remember it and aint ashamed of it." Anderson reminded him, "You're a country boy; all you know is that little patch up there in Mississippi where you started from."[9] Perhaps in recognition of this advice (whether actually articulated or extrapolated from Anderson's work), Faulkner dedicated *Sartoris*, the first published work dealing with "that little patch up there in Mississippi," to Anderson. He also might have had Anderson—or specifically *Winesburg, Ohio*—in mind when, while working on *Flags in the Dust*, he began drafting "a collection of short stories" about his "townspeople" (*L*, p. 34). It is impossible to determine from the available evidence how far he got with this project, or even to know whether "Father Abraham" was initially conceived as a part of the collection, but it obviously was designed specifically to complement his other work on Yoknapatawpha and to contribute to the growing population of his mythical county.[10]

Stone and Anderson pointed the young novelist toward his native region, but the final decision to call his muse home was, of course, Faulkner's own. In a rhapsodic essay on the composition of *Sartoris*, he describes the effect of this decision, explaining how the aesthetic discovery of his native environment stemmed from a profoundly personal sense of mutability and loss. "One day" while "speculating idly upon time and death," the piece begins, he realized that "the simple bread-and-salt of the world," as he "had found it in the finding years," was rapidly passing into oblivion, and that having been

> previously under the curse of words, having known twice
> before the agony of ink, nothing served but that I try by main
> strength to recreate between the covers of a book the world
> I was already preparing to lose and regret, feeling, with the
> morbidity of the young, that I was not only on the verge of
> decrepitude, but that growing old was to be an experience pe-
> culiar to myself alone out of all the teeming world, and desir-
> ing, if not the capture of that world and the fixing of it, as
> you'd preserve a kernel or a leaf, to indicate the lost forest, at
> least to keep the evocative skeleton of the desiccated leaf.
>   So I began to write, without much purpose, until I realized
> that to make it truly evocative it must be personal, in order
> to not only preserve my own interest in the writing, but to
> preserve my belief in the savor of the bread-and-salt. . . . So
> I got some people, some I invented, others I created out of
> tales I learned of nigger cooks and stable boys. . . . Created I
> say, because they are composed partly from what they were
> in actual life and partly from what they should have been and
> were not.[11]

Creatively confronting his own time and place thus appears to have been as much a private gesture of mnemonic re-creation as an act of aesthetic invention. In seeking to preserve the "evocative skeleton" of a world that was swiftly and inexorably fading, Faulkner looked toward his native region with a new eye and tapped previously unexplored imaginative resources.

In July 1927, having drafted a substantial portion of *Flags in the Dust*, he enthusiastically told Liveright, his publisher, that this novel was "much better than that other stuff. I believe that at last I have learned to control the stuff and fix it on something like rational truth" (*L*, p. 37). This new sense of artistic control no doubt derived from the markedly personal nature of the novel's subject matter, for a good deal of the "rational truth" on which *Flags in the Dust* is "fixed" stems directly from the author's experience or from inherited family legend. Taken as a whole, as numerous critics have pointed out, *Flags in the Dust* probably contains more local and autobiographical material than any other work in the Faulkner canon. Not only does the novel's setting accurately reflect the specific geographical and cultural features of Faulkner's homeland, but the major representatives of the Sartoris family, as Faulkner himself admitted, are modeled closely on members of the Faulkner (or Falkner) clan[12]—including the novelist's great-grandfather, grandfather, and great-aunt—and other characters, such as Simon Strother, Will Falls, and the Doctors Peabody and Alford had identifiable prototypes among his Oxford neighbors. [13]

Conrad had stated that "every novelist must begin by creating for himself a world, great or little, in which he can honestly believe";[14] Faulkner, having decided to reexamine his native roots, quickly discovered that his personal experience of north Mississippi could be transformed into precisely that kind of fictional world. "I wrote *Soldiers' Pay* and *Mosquitoes*," Faulkner later stated, "for the sake of writing because it was fun. But I found out after that not only each book had to have a design but the whole output or sum of an artist's work had to have a design. . . . I discovered that my own little postage stamp of native soil was worth writing about and that I would never live long enough to exhaust it, and by sublimating the actual into apocryphal I would have complete liberty to use whatever talent I might have to its absolute top. It opened up a gold mine of other peoples, so I created a cosmos of my own" (*LG*, p. 255). Yoknapatawpha was thus initially conceived as one of Conrad's "great" worlds, as a complete fictional "cosmos" extending beyond the covers of a single work. It was able to accommodate the full range of Faulkner's imaginative vision without sacrificing his overriding sense of aesthetic form.

This concentration on a single imaginative world is, of course, not without literary precedents: as Michael Millgate points out, Yoknapatawpha has much in common with Wessex, Thomas Hardy's fictional domain, especially with regard to its regional setting and provincial perspective.[15] Like Hardy, Faulkner focuses on an isolated, rural, and culturally backward community, distanced geographically, economically, and even morally, from the complex society of the author's sophisticated and predominantly urban readership. In Yoknapatawpha, as in Wessex, men follow simple "earthbound" lives, and natural cycles and inherited traditions remain strong motivating forces, which contribute significantly to characterization and action alike.

For all its regional characteristics and demonstrable correspondences to Wessex, however, Yoknapatawpha more closely parallels the universe of Honoré de Balzac's *Comédie humaine* in its overall shape and organizational design. Faulkner's imaginative world, like Balzac's but unlike Hardy's, is fundamentally an interlocking structure, where narratives overlap, characters reappear, and there is substantial cross-referencing between texts. These manifold intersections and repetitions work to interrelate the individual Yoknapatawpha novels, creating a kind of comprehensive fictional construct that draws on a common population, occupying a common region, sharing common customs, and participating in a common history. Many years after the inception of Yoknapatawpha, Faulkner praised Balzac's formidable achievement by specifically calling attention to the inclusive design of his "intact world," a world where characters "don't just move from page one to page 320 of one book," but rather where there "is continuity between them all like a blood-stream which flows from page one through to page 20,000 of one book. The same blood, muscle and tissue binds the characters together" (*LG*, p. 217). Faulkner was attempting to create in Yoknapatawpha precisely this kind of integrated yet infinitely expandable world. Although it is impossible to determine whether, as Phil Stone suggests, he was deliberately patterning the structure of his fictional domain on the *Comédie humaine*, his previous reliance on "masters" and formal models points in that direction.[16]

In 1927, working simultaneously on *Flags in the Dust* and on "Father Abraham" and the "stories" of his "towns-people," Faulkner made his first attempt to realize this imaginative world on paper. From its very inception, the regional, Hardyan focus and the interrelated, Balzacian design are evident. Alternating between his several Yoknapatawpha (or Yocona) projects, Faulkner not only sketched in the entire ground plan of his mythical county—providing a comprehensive picture of its social, topographic, and demographic range—but also, through cross-referencing and allusion, indicated the interdependent nature of its underlying pattern. In *Flags in the Dust*, for example, in order to describe more fully the rapidly changing face of Jefferson society and help characterize Horace Benbow's obnoxious YMCA comrade, Montgomery Ward Snopes, Faulkner provides a summary of much of the material that appears in "Father Abraham":

This Snopes was a young man, member of a seemingly inexhaustible family which for the last ten or twelve years had been moving to town in driblets from a small settlement known as Frenchman's Bend. Flem, the first Snopes, had appeared

unheralded one day and without making a ripple in the town's
life, behind the counter of a small restaurant on a side street,
patronized by country people. With this foothold and like
Abraham of old, he led his family piece by piece into town.
Flem himself was presently manager of the city light and water
plant, and for the following few years he was a sort of handy-
man to the city government; and three years ago, to old Bayard
Sartoris' profane surprise and unconcealed disapproval, he
became vice-president of the Sartoris bank, where already a
relation of his was a book-keeper. [*FD*, p. 154]

Aside from providing early evidence of the comprehensive nature of Yoknapatawpha's larger structural design, this
short passage reveals another significant characteristic of
Faulkner's fictional world. For all its regional specificity and
mimetic accuracy, Yoknapatawpha is fundamentally a symbolic "cosmos," an imaginative "sublimation" of the "actual." The Snopeses, for example, despite their exaggerated,
almost Dickensian, idiosyncrasies, remain essentially representative figures, typical in some degree of an entire class
of recently emergent tenant farmers. And Faulkner chroni-
cles their genesis and symbolic migration to Jefferson with
a kind of neutral detachment, demonstrating little regard for
causal explanation or narrative plausibility, presenting the
results rather than the means of their mysterious economic
machinations. Flem, in particular, is portrayed more as a
psychological type, a sort of Jonsonian "humour," than as a
fully realized novelistic character. It is even possible that
Faulkner named and modeled the taciturn, unscrupulous,
and unemotional patriarch of the Snopes clan after the
"phlegmatic temperament" as defined in D. Starke's *Character: How to Strengthen It*, a book from Faulkner's library:

Phlegm is a defense against visible emotion. It is not
hypocrisy or falsehood, for the phlegmatic utter no sentiment
contrary to that which they fill. They are content not to let

anything transpire of the cause of their agitation. One may compare a phlegmatic man to a thick veil under which the play of the features, and under this the acts of the mind, are dissembled.

Hypocrisy resembles a dead wall covered with lying advertisements.

Phlegm is this dead wall wholly denuded of these. We can conjecture what it conceals, but in no case can we accuse it of saying anything contrary to truth.[17]

Sometime in the early summer of 1927, after having delineated the general features of Frenchman's Bend and the surrounding environs, firmly implanted the Snopeses in Jefferson, and introduced a good portion of the county's rural population—the Varners, MacCallums, Turpins, Littlejohns, and the Quicks—Faulkner temporarily put aside "Father Abraham" and its related materials to concentrate on the completion of *Flags in the Dust*. Though, as some critics have suggested, he may have chosen to abandon "Father Abraham" in favor of *Flags in the Dust* simply because the Sartoris material was more familiar to him, the inherently broader social and chronological scope of the latter text may also have been a determining factor.[18] It is very possible that Faulkner decided to continue with *Flags in the Dust* precisely because its panoramic structure afforded him a better opportunity to establish and expand his fictional world and thus provide himself with a solid foundation for future development. Faulkner may have also seen *Flags in the Dust* as having greater commercial potential than "Father Abraham," and it is not unlikely that this novel, like *Mosquitoes* before it, was written with one eye toward the marketplace—as, indeed, Faulkner's letters and contemporary statements seem to suggest (*L*, pp. 37–39). In any case, it appears that Faulkner worked almost exclusively on *Flags in the Dust* throughout the summer and early fall of 1927, finishing the 596-page typescript on September 29.

On completing the novel Faulkner was confident of its
future success, aesthetic and commercial, and was therefore
totally unprepared for Liveright's devastating rejection—"It
is diffuse and non-integral with neither very much plot development nor character development . . . we don't believe
that you should offer it for publication."[19] He clung for a
time to the hope that it was still marketable. After various
attempts at revision and numerous subsequent refusals,
however, Faulkner "got a little weary of it" (L, p. 41) and
allowed Ben Wasson, his friend and literary agent, to place
it with Harcourt Brace, despite their insistence that it be
substantially abridged and retitled "Sartoris."[20] Since Faulkner initially "refused to have anything to do with" the cutting, Harcourt hired Wasson to edit the text.[21] Thus was
begun the much discussed but still obscure process of deletion and revision by which the Flags in the Dust typescript
was transformed into Sartoris.

With the evidence presently available, it is impossible to
determine exactly what role Faulkner played in the editing,
to be certain whether he was personally responsbile for the
various passages in Sartoris that do not appear in the surviving Flags in the Dust typescript (the one from which the
book was purportedly published).[22] Nor can it be ascer-
tained what stage of the text this typescript represents, whether
it corresponds to the abandoned one Faulkner himself judged
to be "almost incoherent" (L, p. 41). Nevertheless, there
has been a great deal of critical commentary on the trans-
mission of the text and the differences between the two
versions.[23] A comparison of the texts reveals that the major
alterations involved the deletion of much of the Benbow
and Snopes material, the cutting and rearrangement of certain sections, and a general pruning of descriptive detail.
Basically, these revisions were oriented toward formal concentration and concision—for, as Wasson told Faulkner, the
original version was overcrowded and disorganized: "The

trouble is . . . you had about six books in here. You were trying to write them all at once."[24] Wasson thus accurately pinpointed the underlying difficulty. Rather than having no story to tell, as Liveright contended, *Flags in the Dust* has too many stories to tell.[25] In his first sustained effort to establish his fictional cosmos, Faulkner focused on too many families, introduced too many characters, offered too many lines of action, and provided far too much descriptive detail. In his haste to preserve the "evocative skeleton" of a world that was rapidly vanishing, he committed what Warren Beck has called the "gifted neophyte's typical error": he let the power of inspiration outrun his sense of structural proportion and "tried to seize at once upon the whole of his opportunity, to let none of it escape, though he had not taken full command of any of it."[26]

A diffuse and chaotic structure, occasionally turgid and prolix language, and an essential lack of focus are, by general agreement, among the consequences of Faulkner's overambitious attempt to articulate the full breadth of his imaginative vision in a single work. But there was a considerable price to be paid for solving these difficulties, at least for solving them in the manner chosen by Wasson. By drastically subordinating the Benbow and Snopes plots, tying off loose ends, and deleting extraneous materials, a more consistent focus on the actions and destinies of the Sartoris clan was certainly achieved. Yet, as critics have pointed out, the overall effect of these revisions was a diminution rather than a simplification of the original design. The cutting, for example, fundamentally disturbed the novel's internal balance—the central counterpoint between Bayard and Horace—and disrupted its pattern of character interaction, most notably in the case of the relationship between Horace and Narcissa.[27] The revision also significantly altered the social and demographic scope of the novel: in *Flags in the Dust*, as compared to *Sartoris*, the reader will find more of Yoknapatawpha life, particularly with respect to its cultural and economic diversity.[28]

Although certainly less concentrated and coherent than *Sartoris*, *Flags in the Dust* not only exhibits a more satisfactory formal design—one undoubtedly closer to Faulkner's intentions—but it also represents a much better introduction to the expansive fictional world that Faulkner was attempting to create. Faulkner himself viewed the novel precisely in these terms, and on first examining Wasson's revisions, he forcibly reasserted the essential soundness of his original, more inclusive conception: "I realized for the first time that I had done better than I knew, and the teeming world I had had to create opened before me and I felt myself surrounded by the limbo in which the shady visions of the host which stretched half formed, waiting each with its portion of that verisimilitude which is to bind into a whole the world which for some reason I take it should not pass utterly out of the memory of man."[29] Perhaps more than anything else, *Flags in the Dust* functions as a foundation for this "teeming world," providing—by means of the sheer quantity of Yoknapatawpha materials it contains—a preview of, and storehouse for, the densely imagined fictional domain that would occupy its creator for the remainder of his career.

The characterization in *Flags in the Dust* points toward much of Faulkner's future work. Almost every major figure in the novel reappears in some form or other in subsequent texts and, viewed statistically, *Flags in the Dust* probably introduces more members of the Yoknapatawpha community than any other work in the entire canon. It marks the first appearance of the extensive Sartoris and Snopes families, who go on to play such important roles in *The Unvanquished*, *The Hamlet*, *The Town*, *The Mansion*, and numerous short stories; it also introduces Horace and Narcissa Benbow, who figure prominently in a number of later works, including *Sanctuary* and "There Was a Queen." The

MacCallums, Doc Peabody and V. K. Suratt—prototype for V. K. Ratliff—also make their debut in *Flags in the Dust*, as do a number of less notable local figures to whom Faulkner subsequently returned, such as Dr. Alford, Mrs. Beard, Buck Conners, and the Sartoris retainers—Simon, Caspey, Louvinia, and Isom.

These characters, taken together, represent an extremely broad and varied segment of Yoknapatawpha life, and it seems clear that in *Flags in the Dust* Faulkner deliberately set out to fill in as much of his mythical county's social structure as possible. The intricate portrayal of Jeffersonian society, which focuses on the established Sartoris and Benbow families (and their black servants), the nouveaux riches Mitchells, and the prolific Snopeses, is contrasted to and complemented by an equally elaborate presentation of Yoknapatawpha's rural community, which includes tenant farmers, such as Hub and the black family with whom Bayard spends Christmas, as well as economically independent hillfolk like the MacCallums. The various classes, moreover, are differentiated by means of an extremely detailed depiction of their distinguishing social and cultural characteristics. For example, Faulkner not only offers a lavish description of the Sartoris's opulent Thanksgiving dinner (which, incidentally, provides an elaborate inventory of Yoknapatawpha's game and produce) but also, and with equal attention to particulars, describes the less bountiful Christmas meal at the black sharecropper's cabin. A substantial portion of the novel, in fact, seems directed solely toward the accurate rendering of the community's customs and rituals. There are vivid descriptions of tea parties and possum hunts, of tennis matches and the rites of molasses making, of piano recitals and catfish angling. *Flags in the Dust* thus posits an exceptionally dense and diverse region that can be seen as supplying source materials for the entire range of Faulkner's subsequent Yoknapatawphan productions and as anticipating the various social and cultural worlds of such works as *The Sound and the Fury, As I Lay Dying, Sanctuary*, and *Go Down, Moses.*

Yoknapatawpha's physical characteristics are rendered with a similar attention to detail and a similar concern for the region's geographical and architectural variety. Faulkner portrays the fertile "upland country" of "gums and locusts and massed vines" which leads to the "good broad fields" of Bayard Sartoris's valley (*FD*, p. 9), as well as the less picturesque parts of the county, where "waist high jimson weeds" and "ragged ill-tended fields" surround small "weathered" houses and "gaunt" grey barns (*FD*, pp. 122–23). The depiction of Hub's dilapidated farm, where Suratt takes Bayard after his fall from the stallion, runs for several pages and contains lengthy passages of minutely detailed description: "The earth about the spring was trampled smooth and packed as an earthen floor. Near the spring a blackened iron pot sat on four bricks, beneath it was a heap of pale wood ashes and a litter of extinct brands and charred fagot-ends. Against the pot leaned a scrubbing board with a ridged metal face polished to a dull even gleam like old silver, and a rusty tin cup hung from a nail in the beech tree above the spring" (*FD*, p. 124).

A correspondingly scrupulous concentration on particulars marks the delineation of Jefferson, and *Flags in the Dust* contains numerous scenes that seem designed primarily to evoke the town's specific character and ambience. One street, for example, "bordered by negro stores of one story and shaded by metal awnings," contains "W. C. BEARDS MILL" (*FD*, p. 150); another, across from the square, houses the Beard Hotel, "a rectangular frame building with a double veranda" (*FD*, p. 95), and in the square itself, near the Sartoris bank and the porticoed courthouse with its monument of the Confederate soldier, stands Deacon's "half grocery and confectionery, and half restaurant," with its private

room ("or rather a large disused closet") where reliable customers can surreptitiously concoct and imbibe toddies (*FD*,
p. 110). Typical Jeffersonian sights and sounds are presented with similar care, and much space is devoted to describing such significant features of the local environment
as "a blind negro beggar with a guitar and a wire frame
holding a mouthorgan to his lips" playing "a plaintive reiteration of rich monotonous chords" (*FD*, p. 108); the
drowsing "city fathers" dressed in "the grey of Jackson and
Beauregard and Johnston" (*FD*, p. 149); and the loafing
young men, "pitching dollars or tossing baseballs back and
forth or lying on the grass until the young girls in their little
colored dresses and cheap nostalgic perfume came trooping
down town through the late afternoon to the drug store"
(*FD*, p. 149).

Although there are sections of Faulkner's earlier novels
that accurately render surface detail, even the most realistic
of these contain little that would prepare one for that persistent concentration on the social and regional context which
is everywhere apparent in *Flags in the Dust*. As the novel
progresses, such passages as those describing the Sartoris's
Thanksgiving dinner, Hub's farm, or the Jefferson street
scenes work cumulatively to create an intensely realized
image of a specific landscape, a specific town, and a specific
culture at a specific moment in time—an image whose importance extends far beyond *Flags in the Dust* to the whole
subsequent development of Yoknapatawpha.

Faulkner's novelistic domain was conceived as an entire
cosmos, a comprehensive and interrelated imaginative
structure. In this first Yoknapatawpha novel, therefore, he
wanted to create not merely a fictional world but a fictional
world to which he could return. *Flags in the Dust*, with its
large cast, social range, chronological scope, and panoramic structure, established precisely that kind of world.
Although shifting slightly from text to text, the geographical

and cultural dimensions of Yoknapatawpha remained substantially the same at the end of Faulkner's career as when first depicted in *Flags in the Dust*: Lucius Priest and Gavin Stevens walk the same streets as Bayard Sartoris and Horace Benbow; Miss Habersham and Byron Snopes drive the same country roads; the MacCallums and the McCaslins share virtually the same attitudes toward hunting and the land; and Temple Drake Stevens and Narcissa Benbow exploit the same facade of "Southern womanhood."

A number of the dominant themes and motifs of Faulkner's elaborated fictional world are also introduced in *Flags in the Dust*. It is, for example, the first novel in which he dramatizes the decline of a long-established and formerly influential Southern family ("De Sartorises set de quality in dis country" as Simon puts it), a subject that he would subsequently reexplore in various contexts and that would be seen by some critics as central to the shape and design of his whole literary output.[30] *Flags in the Dust* also marks Faulkner's initial attempt to deal with the historical past—specifically the past of the Civil War—and the living legacy of that past, the succession of generations through which its experiences are codified and transmitted. Furthermore, it introduces the more complex and more typically Faulknerian question—asked above all in *Absalom, Absalom!* and *Go Down, Moses*—about the way in which present action is affected and impinged on by the past.

History and heredity play major roles in *Flags in the Dust* as they had not done in Faulkner's previous novels, and this text, which contains no less than three Bayards and two Johns, is the first in which Faulkner emphatically reduplicates his characters' Christian names, a strategy to which he would return in *The Sound and the Fury* and other works centered on the fortunes of an individual family. This kind of repetition not only demonstrates a move away from the traditional notion of autonomous characters, as certain critics have pointed out, but it also calls attention to those features that interrelate different generations and thus stresses the shaping and sustaining forces of genealogy and posterity.[31] The themes of history and heredity, moreover, are specifically united in the characterization of young Bayard, who carries the weight of the legendary Sartoris past as well as the Sartoris genes. It is perhaps an indication of Faulkner's fascination with these subjects that he chose to add familial guilt and racial destiny to a self-destructive psyche already overburdened with scars from a recent war,[32] severed ties of twinship, and other indications of what T. H. Adamowski has diagnosed as classical symptoms of "Mourning and Melancholia."[33]

Flags in the Dust also touches on such typically Faulknerian topics as family breakdown, past-obsession, self-destructiveness (in Bayard and Horace), lovelessness (in Bayard and Narcissa), parentlessness (in the Benbow as well as the Sartoris families), and incest (in the Horace-Narcissa relationship). It indeed offers an extensive introduction to some of the major themes Faulkner was to return to again and again during his subsequent career. Overambitious, overextended, and insufficiently focused though it is, *Flags in the Dust* derives strength from the sense of excitement Faulkner obviously felt at this first discovery of the world, the people, and, in some degree, the themes that were to constitute his lifelong subject. If his previous novel, *Mosquitoes*, can be seen as a kind of compendium or anthology of his past, *Flags in the Dust* offers what is in effect a prospectus for his future.

Not everything in *Flags in the Dust*, however, points forward. Although in terms of content this novel was so important and necessary an advance, there was no corresponding development in style, structure, or technique. *Flags in the Dust* evokes no new or refurbished ways of organizing or focusing its newly discovered material but relies almost entirely on procedures and strategies that had informed the earlier fiction. It seems almost as though the direct confrontation of the claims of his native environment left him with little energy to devote to questions of aesthetic form. Like its predecessors, for example, *Flags in the Dust* contains much evidence of the influence of other writers. Although a number of the novel's literary borrowings—such as those from Keats's "Ode on a Grecian Urn" (*FD*, pp. 162, 241, 340), Shakespeare's "The Phoenix and the Turtle" (*FD*, p. 53), Tennyson's "Tears, Idle Tears" (*FD*, p. 324), and Kipling's "Recessional" (*FD*, p. 53)—aim at resonant allusion rather than deliberate replication, the majority of the detectable sources exhibit the same kind of formal or stylistic dependency that marked the early apprentice work. The description of Horace's thoughts as he watches his tennis partner, Frankie (*FD*, p. 173), for example, is clearly based on the language, syntax, and imagery of portions of the "Nausicaa" section of Joyce's *Ulysses*. And although this passage may be consciously parodic in intent, as Millgate tentatively suggests,[34] there can be no comparable justification for the inclusion—let alone the appropriation—of Caspey's extravagant and almost vaudevillian depiction of the part he played in saving "France f'um de Germans" (*FD*, pp. 52–57), for this tasteless, obtrusive, and ultimately unassimilated episode constitutes a close reworking of sections of Hugh Wiley's *The Wildcat*, an obscure, frankly racist novel devoted to the European misadventures of a black World War I draftee.[35]

Richard T. Dillon, in "Some Sources for Faulkner's Version of the First Air War," provides what is an even more dramatic, if perhaps less damaging, example of the derivativeness of at least some portions of *Flags in the Dust*.[36] Although James Warner Bellah's "Blood," which appeared in the *Saturday Evening Post* while *Flags in the Dust* was being drafted, may not be the "principal source" for Faulk-

ner's novel, as Dillon contends, there are enough correspondences between the two works to suggest that Faulkner may
have indeed drawn on Bellah's story for characterization and
action. Not only does "Blood" concern the wartime exploits
of a despairing young aviator whose twin brother had been
killed in combat, it depicts an aerial battle in terms very
close to those in which Johnny Sartoris's death is described.
It is also possible that Bayard's "doomed fatality" owes
something, though much less directly, to *Moby-Dick*, which
Faulkner spoke of in July 1927 as the story of "a man of
forceful character driven by his sombre nature and his bleak
heritage, bent on his own destruction and dragging his immediate world down with him with a despotic and utter
disregard of them [*sic*] as individuals."[37] Bayard, of course,
never reaches the tragic heights or Gothic proportions of
Ahab, yet the dramatization of his "bleak and haunted"
despair—"the isolation of that doom he could not escape"—bears a distinct if distant resemblance to Melville's
work.[38] It has also been argued that the poignant molasses-
making interlude in chapter 4, section 1 (*FD*, p. 269), contains "passages which are strong echoes" of Sherwood
Anderson's short story, "A Meeting South."[39] In this case,
however, it seems at least as probable that Faulkner was the
originator, and that Anderson based his episode on materials
he had picked up from the younger writer, especially since
Faulkner himself provided the model for the character in
Anderson's story who relates the incident in question.

Flags in the Dust also shows Faulkner's continued dependence on his literary past. There are, for example, distinct
parallels between the "central situation" of *Flags in the Dust*
and that of *Soldiers' Pay*,[40] and just as the dying Donald in
that first novel "is set off against the dead Donald of the
past," so the "dying" Bayard in *Flags in the Dust* "is likewise contrasted with Johnny, his dead twin brother."[41] Both
works, moreover, deal with the dual themes of sex and

death, and in *Flags in the Dust* the protagonist's gradual
move toward the grave is once again juxtaposed to what
André Bleikasten has called a "tragicomic *chassé-croisé* of
amorous pursuits: love rejected (Bayard-Narcissa), love as
bondage (Benbow-Belle Mitchell), incestuous love (Benbow-
Narcissa), and sheer lust (Byron Snopes-Narcissa)."[42] Other
more specific materials from previous works also found their
way into *Flags in the Dust*. The portrayal of Horace Benbow, for instance, owes a great deal to the presentation of
George Bleyth in "Elmer," and Faulkner did not hesitate to
reuse large portions of that abandoned text for his description of Horace's stay at Oxford.[43]

More important, however, than Faulkner's reliance on
incidents, situations, and characters from his past is his
return to previously tested formal patterns and narrative
techniques. Like *Soldiers' Pay*, that earlier novel about the
plight of recently demobilized veterans, *Flags in the Dust*
opens in the spring of 1919 (the first spring following World
War I) and, through a similar emphasis on the gradually
changing flora and fauna, develops a temporal structure that
is likewise based on the slow progression of the seasons.
This underlying framework of seasonal movement works
narratively, as a register of the passage of time, and thematically, as a persistent symbol of nature's permanency against
which the temporary disruptions of the war's aftermath are
presented. As in *Soldiers' Pay*, so in *Flags in the Dust*,
Faulkner sets up the central action in such a way that the
protagonist's inevitable motion toward death is dramatically
counterpointed against the evocation of a burgeoning spring.
Donald Mahon's death is thus preceded by an elaborate
image of vernal maturation: "And so April became May.
There were fair days when the sun, becoming warmer and
warmer, rising, drank off the dew, and flowers bloomed like
girls ready for a ball, then drooped in the langourous ful-
some heat like girls after the ball; when earth, like a fat

woman, recklessly trying giddy hat after hat, trying a trim-
ming of apple . . . and jonquil and flag: threw it away—so
early flowers bloomed and passed and later flowers bloomed
to fade and fall, giving place to yet later ones" (*SP*, p. 281).

In the final pages of *Flags in the Dust*, a similar insistence
on seasonal change serves as a prelude to young Bayard's
death: "Then it was definitely spring again. Miss Jenny's
and Isom's annual vernal altercation began, continued its
violent but harmless course in the garden. . . . Narcissa
drove into town, saw the first jonquils on the now deserted
lawn, blooming as though she and Horace were still there,
and later, the narcissi. But when the gladioli bloomed she
was not going out any more save in the late afternoon or
early evening, when she and Miss Jenny walked in the garden among burgeoning bloom and mockingbirds and be-
lated thrushes where the long avenues of gloaming sunlight
reluctant leaned" (*FD*, p. 351).

Faulkner also depends on his previous experience for solutions to the organizational problems caused by the overcrowded cast and multistranded plot of his first
Yoknapatawpha novel. Like *Soldiers' Pay* and *Mosquitoes*,
Flags in the Dust is divided into numerous sections and
subsections, and there is the same abrupt cutting from scene
to scene and incident to incident with little regard for transition or narrative summation. Within the space of four pages
(*FD*, pp. 240–44), Faulkner rapidly juxtaposes episodes
dealing with Bayard and Narcissa's romance, Horace and
Belle's marriage, and Byron Snopes's lust, deploying precisely the same montage techniques that he had used in
Soldiers' Pay (for example, *SP*, pp. 184–87) and *Mosquitoes* (for example, *M*, pp. 201–3). This essentially scenic
method of narrative exposition lends itself readily to the
presentation of simultaneous action, and in *Flags in the
Dust*, as in *Soldiers' Pay*, Faulkner resorts to this strategy
in an attempt to unify some of the novel's diverse materials.

Just as the temporal alignment of Cecily's tryst and Mahon's homecoming in chapter 2 of *Soldiers' Pay* served to join the pre- and post-war plots, so the insistence on the simultaneous occurrence of Bayard's serenade, Narcissa's disrupted sleep, and Byron Snopes's surreptitious visit effectively connects some of the otherwise divergent plot lines in *Flags in the Dust*. The formal design and verbal texture of *Flags in the Dust* may also owe something to the elaborate network of deliberately repeated motifs in *Soldiers' Pay*, for while the later novel offers no instances of verbal reiteration as obvious as the pigeon or tree imagery of *Soldiers' Pay*, such passages as those centered on the "dying fall" of music (*FD*, pp. 37, 157, 370), "sourceless" sensations (*FD*, pp. 36, 42, 240), and the "myriad" scent of flowers (*FD*, pp. 10, 47, 76, 102) create recurrent patterns that are undoubtedly designed to serve larger structural functions.[44]

Faulkner's use of language in *Flags in the Dust* also points backward rather than forward, and the novel reflects the kind of deliberate stylistic heterogeneity that characterized *Soldiers' Pay* and *Mosquitoes*. Like these earlier works, *Flags in the Dust* contains an impressive range of narrative styles: alongside intensely detailed descriptive passages, such as those recording the minutiae of Old Bayard's "office" (*FD*, p. 30)—which may be indebted as much to the tradition of American realism (as embodied in the work of Twain and Howells) as to Balzac—one finds self-conscious set pieces (such as the celebrated encomium of the mule), Old Man Falls's vernacular reminiscences, and dramatizations of Horace's decadent consciousness.[45] One might also include the highly ornate evocations of the legendary Sartoris past, such as the account of the Carolina Bayard's coffee raid, in which "a hair-brained prank of two heedless and reckless boys wild with their own youth" becomes rhetorically transformed into "a gallant and finely tragical focal-point to which the history of the race had been raised from

out the old miasmic swamps of spiritual sloth by two angels
valiantly and glamorously fallen and strayed, altering the
course of human events and purging the souls of men" (*FD*,
p. 12).

Although these distinctive styles do not invariably reflect
the central concerns of *Flags in the Dust*, differences in
language and voice frequently do serve narrative functions,
as they had done in *Soldiers' Pay* and were to do in the
future. In particular, the richly embellished prose style used
to describe the adventures of young Bayard's forebears effectively distinguishes the nineteenth-century Sartorises from
their less glamorous progeny and forcibly emphasizes the
romantic appeal of the "old dead pattern" that the Sartoris
family had so dramatically established. Although the manner of Johnny's death seems almost as impetuous and certainly as foolhardy as that of the Carolina Bayard, it is
significant, especially in terms of the sustaining Sartoris
rhetoric, that it is recalled in language "crassly and uselessly
violent and at times profane and gross" (*FD*, p. 238) and is
thus distanced, rhetorically and ethically, from that florid
assessment of his ancestor's final exploit quoted above. Even
though young Bayard often talks about it, Johnny's death
never becomes transmuted into the finer fabric of legend,
and he is last seen jumping from the disabled plane, thumb-
ing his nose at his brother. The Carolina Bayard, on the
other hand, is twice eulogized, and he leaves the novel in
what amounts to a romantic apotheosis: he becomes a flam-
ing star "garlanded with Fame's burgeoning laurel and the
myrtle and roses of Death" (*FD*, p. 13) or, again, "a shooting star . . . with a transient glare like a soundless thunder-
clap, leaving a sort of radiance when it died" (*FD*, p. 19).

The abbreviated text published as *Sartoris* opens with this
kind of highly poetical language, which is designed to invoke from the start the "palpable presence" of the legendary
Sartoris past—"the creatures of that prehistoric day that

were too grandly conceived and executed either to exist very long or to vanish utterly when dead from an earth shaped and furnished for punier things."[46] *Flags in the Dust*, however, begins with a vernacular tale narrated by Old Man Falls.[47] Although abrupt and at first confusing, this is not only a more dramatic and arresting opening than that of *Sartoris*, but it harks back to the strategies of *Soldiers' Pay*. Like that first novel, *Flags in the Dust* begins with a kind of narrative tour de force—a headlong rush into the heart of the Sartoris myth. As the first chapter develops, other stories of the Sartoris past (Bayard's mnemonic re-creation and the Christmas tale) merge with Old Man Falls's narrative to provide a varied sampling of the family's legendary exploits. Yet, given the disconcerting immediacy of the actual opening, the plunge directly into the oral tale, and the rapid run through the Sartoris genealogy, it takes a good while before the reader has sorted out the three Bayards, two Johns, and two "Cunnels" and made sense of the various interpolated stories. The emphasis in these early scenes, therefore, falls on a general delineation of those qualities that serve to define the Sartoris past, and there is very little attempt to initiate the plot or introduce the major characters. Rather than setting the traditional novelistic machinery in motion, the opening of *Flags in the Dust* thus functions (like that of *Soldiers' Pay*) as a kind of thematic prelude in which narrative exposition is subordinated to a preview of the central tensions (notably, that between a legendary past and a restricted present) that are to underlie subsequent development.

The ending of *Flags in the Dust* is again dependent on previously explored techniques in that the juxtaposition of Bayard's death and Benbow Sartoris's birth closely corresponds to the positive/negative closural formula that informed the conclusion of *Soldiers' Pay*. The birth/death motif, with its simultaneous emphasis on the completion of the past and the open possibilities of the future, distinctly parallels the alternation of the black church service, with its evocations of a hopeful apotheosis, and the unalterable "facts of division and death," as represented by Gilligan and the rector. In the final paragraphs of *Flags in the Dust*, more-over, Faulkner once again provides the force of closure through linguistic and rhetorical means rather than through the termination of action or the resolution of dominant narrative tensions:

> The dusk was peopled with ghosts of glamorous and old di-sastrous things. And if they were just glamorous enough, there would be a Sartoris in them, and then they were sure to be disastrous. Pawns. But the Player and the game He plays— who knows? He must have a name for his pawns, though, but perhaps Sartoris is the name of the game itself—a game out-moded and played with pawns shaped too late and to an old dead pattern, and of which the Player Himself is a little wea-ried. For there is death in the sound of it, and a glamorous fatality, like silver pennons downrushing at sunset, or a dying fall of horns along the road to Roncevaux. [*FD*, pp. 369–70]

The invocation of a larger and ultimately incomprehensible controlling force ("the Player"), the allusions to an even more glamorously fatal past ("along the road to Ronce-vaux"), the explicitly terminal images ("death," "fatal," "sunset"), and the general movement toward cessation and silence ("downrushing," "dying fall")—all these combine to constitute an adequate verbal closure consistent with Faulkner's previous practices of imposing aesthetically sat-isfying endings on otherwise unresolved narratives. But the values implicit in this kind of romantic determinism ("the old dead pattern") are never examined, and the ending offers no solution to the fundamental problem of how one is to understand and assess the Sartoris myth and its destructive consequences.

The ambiguous ending is merely symptomatic of a more pervasive ambiguity underlying the structure and meaning of the novel as a whole. In *Flags in the Dust*, as Bleikasten points out, "we can never know for sure whether we are intended to regard the Sartorises as the blind victims of their own fantasies and fabrications or as the helpless pawns of a cruel cosmic Player." In the last analysis, Bleikasten continues, "Faulkner's attitude toward the Sartoris myth . . . is ambivalent in a way reminiscent of Miss Jenny's in the novel: even though he is able to see it in the light of irony, he as yet cannot free himself completely from its spell, divided as he himself is at this point between sentimental allegiance to the past and the impulse to question it."[48] This underlying problem is, in part, related to Faulkner's continued reliance on the fictional structures of his past, his inability to find new or renewed ways of giving aesthetic and moral coherence to the fresh materials that this first Yoknapatawpha novel introduced. His use of point of view, for example, does not provide enough depth or detail for the kind of mental disclosure that his subject requires.[49] Although the rudimentary strategies for rendering consciousness that were employed in *Soldiers' Pay* and *Mosquitoes* were adequate for the externalization of Mrs. Powers's repressed guilt or the taciturn Gordon's aesthetic ramblings, the dramatization of Bayard's past-obsessed consciousness needed more innovative methods of internal presentation than Faulkner's technical repertoire could yet provide, and the resulting superficiality and ambivalence of his characterization contributes largely to the fundamental irresolution of the novel itself.

For all its anticipations of Faulkner's future, then, *Flags in the Dust* is essentially retrospective in its style, use of point of view, narrative strategy, and overall formal organization. Although, in terms of content, it unquestionably marks a significant turning point in Faulkner's career—especially with regard to the inception of the imaginative world that was to constitute his central lifelong subject—it reveals no corresponding breakthrough in technique, no discovery of fresh or freshly renovated ways to organize and embody the narrative or thematic components of that world. In his eagerness to articulate his new and exciting fictional domain, Faulkner perhaps did not take the time to let the aesthetic form and narrative techniques grow naturally from his materials, and the novel's diffuseness and overburdened structure is as much a product of his dependence on other writers and his past as of the ambitious scope of his initial imaginative design. Although *Flags in the Dust* did not turn out to be "THE book," as Faulkner had optimistically hoped (*L*, p. 38), it represented a major and indispensable move in the direction he would have to take. It showed him what he would have to leave behind, pointing by negative example toward the kind of dramatic concentration, technical flexibility, and formal innovation that would be necessary for his subsequent development as a novelist.

6.
Quitting Reading
The Sound and the Fury

At the beginning of 1928, Faulkner's literary career had reached a critical stage. *Flags in the Dust*, "THE book" that he believed would make his name for him as a writer had been rejected, the magazines were not buying his short stories, and, to make matters worse, he still owed his publisher a $200 "super-advance," which he had drawn the previous summer (*L*, pp. 38–39). In February he wrote Horace Liveright, his publisher, about his financial and creative predicament, asking for permission to submit *Flags in the Dust* elsewhere and informing him that, in an attempt to repay the debt, he had "just sent some short stories to an agent." If these plans should prove to be commercially unsuccessful, Faulkner continued, "I dont know what we'll do about it, as I have a belly full of writing, now, since you folks in the publishing business claim that a book like that last one I sent you is blah. I think now that I'll sell my typewriter and go to work—though God knows, it's sacrilege to waste that talent for idleness which I possess" (*L*, p. 39).

Faulkner's disillusionment, however, did not last long. Within a few weeks of the letter to Liveright, he was not only energetically working on a new novel, but also experiencing a hitherto unknown feeling of what can only be termed creative euphoria: "that emotion definite and physical and yet nebulous to describe: that ecstasy, that eager and joyous faith and anticipation of surprise which the yet unmarred sheet beneath my hand held inviolate and unfailing, waiting for release."[1] By some obscure process of the imagination, Faulkner's discouragement had been transformed into a new sense of aesthetic freedom. On finally relinquishing the hope of commercial success, he later recalled, "it suddenly seemed as if a door had clapped silently and forever to between me and all publishers' addresses and booklists and I said to myself, Now I can write. Now I can just write."[2] Rather than abandon his typewriter, Faulkner thus abandoned, at least temporarily, the public dimension of his art—those indefinite but restrictive external pressures he thought of as being imposed by publishers and potential readers—and for the first time since *Soldiers' Pay*, perhaps even since *The Marble Faun*, he totally forgot his audience and let his creative impulse flow unchecked.

So, at least, runs Faulkner's retrospective account, which no doubt accurately reflects his feelings at the time; it is worth noting, however, that in Anderson's *A Story Teller's Story*, which Faulkner reviewed in 1925, the narrator expresses practically the same attitude toward publishing and creativity: "When later I began to write I . . . told myself I would never publish, and I remember that I went about thinking of myself as a kind of heroic figure, a silent man creeping into little rooms, writing marvelous tales, poems, novels—that would never be published."[3] Whatever its sources, however, Faulkner's new found sense of expressive liberation resulted in *The Sound and the Fury*, and though he later called into play what he termed the "policeman" of structural "coherence" and order,[4] he insisted that the novel was begun as an entirely private affair, without any preconceived design, with absolutely "no plan at all."[5]

The Sound and the Fury, as Faulkner himself well knew, marked a unique moment in his imaginative life and literary career. It was, above all else, a decisive "turning point." He had already "written three novels, with progressively decreasing ease and pleasure, and reward or emolument,"[6] but with the fourth he not only enjoyed a previously unknown (and subsequently irretrievable) feeling of unalloyed creativity ("that first ecstasy"), but also "discovered that there is actually something to which the shabby term Art not only can, but must, be applied." *The Sound and the Fury*, Faulkner declared in 1933, was the only novel he had written "without any accompanying feeling of drive or effort, or any following feeling of exhaustion or relief or distaste." For in it, he went on to say, "I had already put perhaps the only thing in literature which would ever move me very much: Caddy climbing the pear tree to look in the window at her grandmother's funeral while Quentin and Jason and Benjy and the negroes looked up at the muddy seat of her drawers."[7]

According to Faulkner's description of the novel's inception, *The Sound and the Fury* thus represents important and simultaneous breakthroughs: the realization of new imaginative powers and rewards, the recognition of art, the materialization of a beloved. It represents—as the emphasis on Caddy's role suggests—simply the discovery of his muse.[8] His unbridled excitement at this discovery undoubtedly underlies much of what makes this novel initially seem so radical a departure—in technique, thought, and achievement—from his past. It may also be responsible for the heavy stress Faulkner himself places on the singularity of its genesis, the separation of it from creative experiences that came before or after, and the devaluation of those other works, lest his muse—"the beautiful one" (*FU*, p. 6)— should be provoked to jealously.

There is no doubt that the appearance of *The Sound and*

the Fury was not only unpredictable but, at bottom, inexplicable, and critics, like the author himself, have accorded it a special, almost sacred, status. "What happened to Faulkner between *Mosquitoes* and the novel that came a few years later, *The Sound and the Fury*?" Irving Howe, like Bleikasten,[9] asks: "What element of personal or literary experience can account for such a leap? At the door to this mystery there is no use pretending entry."[10] Yet it should by now be clear that the mystery, though real, is in some respects less awesome than Howe's language suggests. Not only did the earlier work more distinctly anticipate techniques, narrative strategies, and creative procedures used in the composition of this text than has been formerly thought, it also, and more importantly, provided Faulkner with materials and methods to which he could return. The writing of *The Sound and the Fury*, in fact, constituted for Faulkner not so much a mysterious leap as an initiation—what Lawrence Lipking calls "the starting-out, the gathering-in."[11] It marks that crucial point in Faulkner's career at which he revisited his past, saw it afresh, and reworked it into his future.

It has, for example, been shown that Benjy Compson is physically modeled on the unnamed idiot in "The Kingdom of God," one of the sketches Faulkner published in the *Times-Picayune* in 1925.[12] What has not been so fully appreciated is the extent to which the earlier figure gave Faulkner an opportunity to imagine an idiot's inherent perceptual and linguistic limitations and thus to envision the expressive possibilities of a "truly innocent" narrator (*LG*, p. 146). In "The Kingdom of God," the idiot is described as being "utterly vacant of thought," having "life without mind," "an organism without intellect" (*NO*, p. 55), and although all of these epithets accurately define Benjy as he is perceived from the "outside" (in the novel's final three sections), they also can be seen as descriptive of his narrative role in section 1. Every device that contributes to Benjy's radically simplistic narrative voice—the repetitiveness of the diction, the almost exclusive use of active, declarative sentences, the flattening of temporal distinctions, and the disquieting unification of tone—works toward the articulation of "life without mind" and "organism without intellect."[13] In the novel's first section, as numerous critics have pointed out, there is no attempt to place experience within a cause and effect relationship, no subjective ordering process. Benjy, as Faulkner himself put it, speaks "only through his senses" (FU, p. 95); he is "incapable of relevancy" (FU, p. 64); he knows "what happened, but not why" (LG, p. 245). Thus, through a violent denudation of the conventions for presenting normal mental activity, Faulkner artificially creates the inner world of a "true innocent," directly building on his previous work to present "life without mind" in wholly dramatic terms.

It has also been argued that other members of the Compson family are based on characters from Faulkner's literary past. The portrayal of Quentin Compson, for example, undoubtedly owes something to the suicidal knight, Sir Galwyn, from Faulkner's early allegorical fantasy Mayday, as well as to a more direct and immediate predecessor, Horace Benbow of Flags in the Dust.[14] Quentin can in fact be seen as a radically intensified version of Horace—as if in creating him Faulkner had looked back to Horace and translated his debilitating but controllable neuroses into incurable psychoses. Horace's fascination with Narcissa thus becomes Quentin's deadly desire for Caddy, his longing for temporal transcendence becomes Quentin's hopeless "chronophobia," and his disastrous marriage to Belle becomes Quentin's final union with his sister Death.[15]

Caddy Compson may similarly be seen as an imaginative reworking of Jo-Addie Hodge from Faulkner's unfinished novel "Elmer."[16] Like Caddy, Jo-Addie has rather ineffectual parents and three brothers, the youngest of whom, Elmer, is deeply attached to her and (like Caddy's youngest brother, Benjy) frequently shares her bed. Like Caddy, too, Jo-Addie permanently leaves home before this brother can properly understand the loss, leaving behind only a box of crayons, which, like Caddy's satin slipper, becomes transformed into an evocative symbol of her memory.[17] Again, both are sexually active (Jo-Addie is apparently a prostitute for a time) and lead somewhat mysterious lives away from home ("For all [Elmer's family] knew she might be Gloria Swanson or J. P. Morgan's wife").[18] The most significant point of comparison between them, however, relates to the means by which they are narratively presented. Like Caddy, Jo-Addie never actually appears in the novel's present; she exists only in the recorded consciousness of her brother and is thus defined exclusively by his personal perceptions of her. Caddy's portrayal, it is true, is infinitely more subtle and complex than that of Jo-Addie (in *The Sound and the Fury*, after all, all three brothers provide portraits of their absent sister),[19] but there are sufficient correspondences, in subject matter and technique, to indicate that Faulkner's "beautiful one" was not an entirely unique creation.

Faulkner's literary past provided him with more than character prototypes, however, for *The Sound and the Fury* also distinctly builds on specific scenes and episodes from earlier works: the "splinting" of Benjy's narcissus (*SF*, pp. 397–401) is undoubtedly derived from "The Kingdom of God" (*NO*, pp. 59–60), and the scene in which Quentin and the unnamed Italian girl encounter the naked boys swimming by the mill (*SF*, pp. 168–71) is anticipated by chapter 4 of *Soldiers' Pay*, in which Mrs. Powers and Gilligan unexpectedly intrude on a very similar (and similarly unclad) group of young bathers (*SP*, pp. 158–60). Though one episode takes place in Massachusetts, the other in Georgia, they rely on similar settings, sequences of action and imagery. Both open with evocations of slanting sunlight, overheard voices, and "the sound of water." The couple in *Soldiers' Pay* then catches sight of "two wet matted heads spread opening fans of water like muskrats," and the boys Quentin and his companion see have "slick heads" and look "like beavers, the water lipping about their chins." The embarrassed swimmers in both scenes finally take refuge beneath overhanging banks, while the intruders leave the river along curved paths amid intermittent patches of sunlight. The observing adults, moreover, express analogous interest in the humiliated youths' feelings, Mrs. Powers deprecating the silliness of male vanity, repeating "Poor boy" and "I'm sorry I shocked him," and Quentin characteristically emphasizing his companion's feminity, twice exclaiming "Poor kid. You're only a girl."

Quentin's memory of possum hunting with Louis Hatcher (*SF*, p. 142) seems to have been similarly derived from the possum hunt in *Flags in the Dust* (*FD*, pp. 270–75). Like Caspey, the black man in charge of the Sartoris hunt, Louis Hatcher carries a horn "slung on his shoulder" and an old, extremely dirty, and odoriferous lantern. Sharing the same equipment, the two men also share the same language: in both scenes the distant baying of the dogs is punctuated by cries of "Hush, now. Dar he. Whooey" and "Hum, awn, dawg." Furthermore, the two episodes conclude with a similar aural image. In *The Sound and the Fury* the final call to the hounds rings out clear and mellow, as though Louis's "voice were a part of darkness and silence, coiling out of it, coiling into it again," and in *Flags in the Dust* the "sound swelled about them, grave and clear and prolonged, then it died into echoes and so into silence again, leaving no ripple."[20]

That in composing *The Sound and the Fury* Faulkner should borrow materials from such an early and relatively obscure work as "The Kingdom of God" seems quite natural; that he should reuse specific scenes and descriptions from a novel he had only recently completed is more surprising. One might argue that this practice actually substantiates Faulkner's claim that he wrote the novel without any view toward its eventual publication: if he were writing only for himself, it would not matter if he resurrected characters and reworked existing scenes.[21] Or it might be asserted that the assimilated materials constitute psychologically obsessive motifs that habitually recurred in Faulkner's imagination. Still, it must be remembered that precisely this kind of self-borrowing had marked practically all of his previous productions and that in the first of his works which he himself called "Art,"[22] he certainly would not have hesitated to "rob, borrow, beg, or steal from anybody and everybody," least of all from himself, in order "to get the work done" (*LG*, p. 239).

But what is really notable here is the success with which the elements traceable to the earlier works are integrated into the fabric of the later text and operate as intrinsic components of its structure. The description of the idiot's bellowing, for example, was considerably strengthened and expanded: what was portrayed simply as "dreadful sound" and "waves of unbelievable sound" in "The Kingdom of God" became, in the final section of *The Sound and the Fury*, more universally symbolic, eloquent of "the grave hopeless sound of all voiceless misery under the sun" (*SF*, p. 395). More extensive modifications were involved in transforming the discursive possum hunt scene from *Flags in the Dust* into a compressed image of the "violent" yet positive "fecundity" of Quentin's homeland. Here, Faulkner radically condensed the original five-page episode into less than a page without diminishing its essential rhetorical effect (*SF*, p. 140). More importantly, he specifically associated the episode with the section's dominant motifs (light, dark, water, death) by incorporating Louis's superstition regarding his lantern—that cleaning it had saved him from drowning—and by having Quentin's thoughts return to this memory just at the point when he began to "feel the water . . . clear and still in the shadow" of the bridge from which he would later take his life (*SF*, p. 143).

In the swimming episode, again, Faulkner's alteration of the elaborate simile "sun was in the trees like an arrested lateral rain" (*SP*, p. 158) to the simple phrase, "infrequent slanting of sunlight" (*SF*, p. 168), not only made the visual image more concrete but also linked it to other descriptions of the changing angle of the sun—such as the one immediately following the episode, "The sun slanted through to the moss here and there, leveller" (*SF*, p. 171)—and thus contributed to a pattern of temporal motifs serving to chart Quentin's obsession with the passage of time.[23] The association of water with sexuality, which plays such a major role in the larger image structure of section 2,[24] is also clearly present in the reworked swimming scene (the naked youths specifically call attention to the fact that Quentin's symbolic "little sister" is "just a girl") and, taken as a whole, the episode appears to be so entirely and necessarily a part of the overall design of Quentin's monologue that its origins in *Soldiers' Pay* have not surprisingly gone undetected. It is also significant that this scene, with its emphasis on water, adolescence, and rejected female sexuality, is typographically interspersed with—and thus strongly linked to—the extremely important episode involving Natalie, which relies on essentially the same web of associations to dramatize Quentin's adolescent sexual initiation.

Seamlessly integrated into *The Sound and the Fury*, these refurbished scenes show Faulkner learning how to read—and hence reuse—himself. Image complexes and character configurations from earlier texts are reassembled and reinterpreted; previously explored structural patterns and techniques are renovated and put to new uses. It is clear, for instance, that in *The Sound and the Fury* certain strategies and organizational procedures are directly derived from "Elmer," a text that operates primarily by means of lengthy flashbacks specifically keyed to the protagonist's private color associations. In the abandoned novel, as critics have pointed out, Elmer's chromatic sensitivity functions as a structural device, providing a way of suggestively yoking scenes from the past and the present: thus his handling of the red tube of oil paint in book 1 immediately summons up a psychologically significant episode from his childhood—the "red horror" of the night his family's house burned down.[25] Despite the obvious advances in the handling of narrative voice and perspective, scenes from different time periods in *The Sound and the Fury* are related in just this fashion, and Faulkner resorts to a very similar technique for making the temporal transitions: as Elmer's fondling of the red pigment precipitated a flashback to a "red" memory, so Benjy's being "snagged" on the garden fence (*SF*, p. 3) or Quentin's smelling gasoline (*SF*, pp. 213–14) triggers shifts to scenes associated with such experiences in the past. In the timeless world of Benjy's monologue, temporally discrete episodes are juxtaposed almost exclusively in terms of these kinds of interrelationships: the act of walking toward the kitchen with Versh evokes a similar incident with T.P. (*SF*, pp. 44–46); noting the new wheel on the carriage prompts the recollection of an earlier carriage ride (*SF*, pp. 8–9); seeing Quentin and her lover in the swing calls to mind a corresponding episode involving Caddy and Charlie (*SF*, pp. 56–59). Thus, while Benjy's narrative works more dramatically and less abstractly than Elmer's, it is clear that a similar associative framework governs its shape and flow.

The presentation of Quentin's climactic fight scene at the end of the second section of *The Sound and the Fury* is based on dramatic methods of depicting memory which were introduced four years earlier in *Soldiers' Pay*. In chapter 5 of that first novel, Sergeant Madden witnesses a hysterical recruit murder a lieutenant named Powers: "the man . . .

whirled suddenly on the fire-step, his head and shoulders sharp against the sorrowful dawn. 'You got us killed,' he shrieked, shooting the officer in the face at point-blank range" (*SP*, p. 179). A year later, on first meeting Powers's widow, the same battlefield image bursts on Madden's consciousness: " 'Good evening ma'am,' Madden said enveloping her firm, slow hand, remembering a figure sharp against the sky screaming, You got us killed and firing point-blank into another man's face red and bitter in a relief of transient flame against a sorrowful dawn" (*SP*, p. 202). Each subsequent encounter with Mrs. Powers elicits a similar response: the present moment fades from his mind, to be overlaid by the vivid reexperiencing of Powers's violent death. While watching Mrs. Powers drive away from the dance, Madden's thoughts once again obsessively return to the climactic incident: "Powers. A face briefly spitted on the flame of a rifle: a white moth beneath a reluctant and sorrowful dawn" (*SP*, p. 211).

Essentially the same associative strategy underlies the presentation of Quentin's mnemonic re-creation of his struggle with Caddy's lover, Dalton Ames. His Harvard acquaintance, Gerald Bland, is subconsciously identified with Ames, because to Quentin both men appear as aggressively self-confident (and secretly enviable) Lotharios, successful lovers whose cynical, disrespectful attitude toward women— Ames says "theyre all bitches" (*SF*, p. 199), and Bland talks about how they can do nothing "except lie on their backs" (*SF*, p. 207)—offends Quentin's excessively romantic sense of feminine honor.[26] When confronting Bland, Quentin's mind immediately turns to Caddy and Dalton Ames, and he once again compulsively asks, "Did you ever have a sister? did you?" before striking his first ineffectual blows. Just as Madden's meeting with Mrs. Powers called to mind another Powers and caused him to relive the lieutenant's death, so Quentin's quixotic dispute with Bland over feminine virtue causes him to relive his earlier, more personal dispute with Ames.

In both works, the normal passage of time is suspended while attention is focused on the recollected event. Quentin's emotionally charged memory appears (like Madden's) to emerge involuntarily, blotting out present experiences, and Faulkner forcibly underscores this by narrating the bout with Bland only after the remembered episode has been recounted. The entire time Quentin is being "boxed silly" (as Shreve puts it), the reader (and Quentin himself for that matter) is aware only of the past encounter with Ames. But if Quentin's obsessive recollection is like Madden's in obtruding on and dominating ongoing activity, in *The Sound and the Fury* Faulkner goes yet a step further. To emphasize Quentin's pathological preoccupation with the past, he has the Ames fight virtually obliterate the present moment altogether, thus dramatically demonstrating the abnormal degree to which memory controls Quentin's consciousness.

More fundamental structural techniques in *The Sound and the Fury* can also be seen as having been developed from Faulkner's previous work. As his numerous statements on the novel's inception indicate, the decision to open the book with Benjy's monologue, to confront the reader with chaotic, fragmented and ultimately confusing impressions of a mind "incapable of relevancy" (*FU*, p. 64), was not only dictated by the order in which the book was originally drafted—"I wrote the Benjy part first" (*FU*, p. 84)—but also resulted from a deliberate aesthetic choice: "It seemed to me that the book approached nearer the dream if the groundwork of it was laid by the idiot. . . . I shifted those sections back and forth to see where they went best, but my final decision was that though that was not right, that was the best to do it, that was simply the groundwork of that story, as that idiot child saw it" (*FU*, pp. 63–64). Although there is nothing in the opening pages of the earlier fiction as manifestly disconcerting as the presentation of the perceptions of an idiot child, the establishment of the groundwork of a story by immediately assaulting the reader with a formally exaggerated overture to the fictional world he is about to enter had by this time become characteristic of Faulkner's narrative art.

Abrupt, disorienting, and unconventional strategies of exposition are, of course, not exclusively the property of William Faulkner. By the time he came to write *Soldiers' Pay*, novelistic conventions had developed to the point at which a reader was not surprised by certain narrative irregularities, particularly at the book's outset. Indeed, the reader familiar with modern novels frequently expected to participate actively in the initial imaginative construction of the text. But, as Ford Madox Ford was fond of asserting, "openings are . . . of necessity always affairs of compromise";[27] they must strike a balance between stimulating the reader's interest and getting on with the business of the narrative. Beginning fictional texts, as Edward W. Said has pointed out, involves significant psychological and existential questions.[28] Once the problem of establishing origins has been confronted and once the decision to begin has been made, however, the important questions become rhetorical ones: how to engage the reader's attention; how to set up "the rules of the game."[29] Too much initial stimulation, too much irregularity, and too much active participation can result in exasperation rather than engagement. Joyce did not begin *Ulysses* with anything so bewildering as the Proteus episode, nor did Virginia Woolf open *To the Lighthouse* with a scene as complicated as the one dealing with the brown stocking. From the moment he started writing novels, however, Faulkner not only seemed unconcerned about initially disturbing the reader, he habitually made it a point of doing so, and the most confusing passages in the novels that preceded *The Sound and the Fury* commonly fall within the first few pages.

Soldiers' Pay, as we have seen, begins with a rollicking military farce, replete with highly stylized language—a mixture of barracks slang, fractured literary allusions, and verbal absurdities—while *Flags in the Dust* opens with Will Falls's scrambled tale of the Sartoris's legendary exploits, which plunges the reader directly into an almost private recitation of the family myth. As in those earlier novels, it is in the opening section of *The Sound and the Fury* that the reader feels most disoriented. Faulkner once again comes in "without knocking."[30] Instead of beginning with a traditional introductory apparatus—the setting of the scene, the description of the major characters, the initiation of the action, and so forth—he eschews conventional exposition and offers a technical tour de force, directly presenting the curiously formal idiolect of an abnormally limited mind. Just as the disarming burlesque that opens *Soldiers' Pay* and the sequence of recollected "stories" that opens *Flags in the Dust* offer dramatic previews of their texts' central issues, so Benjy's violently jumbled and radically simplistic discourse provides *The Sound and the Fury* with its own distinctive "overture."

It is worth recalling just how disconcerting and defamiliarizing the first paragraph of *The Sound and the Fury* actually is:

> Through the fence, between the curling flower spaces, I could see them hitting. They were coming toward where the flag was and I went along the fence. Luster was hunting in the grass by the flower tree. They took the flag out, and they were hitting. Then they put the flag back and they went to the table, and he hit and the other hit. Then they went on, and I went along the fence. Luster came away from the flower tree and we went along the fence and they stopped and we stopped and I looked through the fence while Luster was hunting in the grass.
> "Here, caddie." He hit. They went away across the pasture. I held to the fence and watched them going away.

"Listen at you, now," Luster said. "Ain't you something. . . . Hush up that moaning." [*SF*, pp. 1–2]

As if to point up the perceptual and syntactical peculiarities
of this opening passage, the final, omnisciently narrated,
section of the novel presents virtually the same scene:

> He took Ben's arm and drew him up and they went to the fence
> and stood side by side there, peering between the matted
> honeysuckle not yet in bloom.
> "Dar," Luster said, "Dar come some. See um?"
> They watched the foursome play onto the green and out,
> and move to the tee and drive. Ben watched, whimpering,
> slobbering. When the foursome went on he followed along the
> fence, bobbing and moaning. One said,[31]
> "Here, caddie. Bring the bag."
> "Hush, Benjy," Luster said, but Ben went on at his sham-
> bling trot, clinging to the fence, wailing in his hoarse, hopeless
> voice. The man played and went on, Ben keeping pace with
> him until the fence turned at right angles, and he clung to the
> fence, watching the people move on and away. [*SF*, p. 394]

Although the later passage can be seen as a kind of "nor-
malized" version of the first, providing an external, authoritative description of Benjy's actions ("curling flower spaces"
= honeysuckle; "hitting" = playing golf; "pasture" = golf
course), it cannot, by itself, throw much light on the more
general significance of the opening scene, the way it symbolically prefigures many of the novel's central concerns.
By the time the reader comes to the last chapter, however,
he is already in a position to perceive retrospectively the
latent implications of that first paragraph.

He has learned, for example, that for Benjy, "caddie"
represents "Caddy," his beloved but long lost sister, and that
the golf course, formerly the Compson pasture, was another
cherished possession that had been taken from him, sold to

pay for his brother Quentin's truncated Harvard education—cut short by his suicide at the end of his first year. The themes of death and loss which underlie the more general presentation of the Compson family's disintegration are thus implicitly present in that opening paragraph, and the remainder of Benjy's section, with its stylistic idiosyncrasies,[32] achronological time scheme, and fragmented exposition, operates in precisely the same fashion—"allowing," as Bleikasten notes, "thematic configurations to emerge much more forcibly than would have been possible within the sequential framework of conventional narration."[33] The entire first section, therefore, can be seen as a kind of thematic prelude,[34] elaborately extrapolated from techniques for opening novels that Faulkner had already explored in his earlier fiction. Benjy, as Faulkner said, "was a prologue like the gravedigger in the Elizabethan dramas. He serves his purpose and is gone" (*LG*, p. 245).

If the creation of Benjy was absolutely crucial to the novel's genesis, his sister Caddy was from the outset its raison d'être and motivating force. "To me," Faulkner stated, "she was the beautiful one, she was my heart's darling. That's what I wrote the book about and I used the tools which seemed to me the proper tools to try to tell, try to draw the picture of Caddy" (*FU*, p. 6). The proper tools that he used to portray Caddy, however, were tools of his own fashioning, ones that he had developed in his earlier works, and they were quite distinct from those usually employed in the delineation of fully realized fictional characters. Because *The Sound and the Fury* was so designed that Caddy never appears in the narrative present and is characterized almost exclusively by means of her brothers' monologues, she emerges as an imprecise and elusive figure, the imaginative product of private impressions and emotionally charged recollections. This strategy not only allowed Faulkner to "draw the picture of Caddy" from different angles, using what were, in effect, different media, it also gave him the opportunity to establish her profound effect on the Compson household in purely dramatic terms. Although the narrative focuses on her and is, in a real sense, controlled by her, she remains a shadowy presence, a representation of unfulfilled desire and loss, and thus functions as a kind of "empty center" around which everything else in the novel revolves.[35] This method of presenting Caddy is rhetorically as well as structurally significant and is entirely consistent with Faulkner's view that "the most beautiful description of anyone . . . is by understatement. . . . It's best to take the gesture, the shadow of the branch, and let the mind create the tree" (*LG*, p. 128). The manner in which he chose to give shape to the "beautiful and tragic story of that doomed little girl" required that his pivotal character should appear essentially as a figure and embodiment of absence, a haunting reflection;[36] Caddy, Faulkner stated, "was still to me too beautiful and too moving to reduce her to telling what was going on . . . it would be more passionate to see her through somebody else's eyes" (*FU*, p. 1).

Although none of his previous creations had affected Faulkner's emotional and imaginative life to the extent that Caddy did, it is clear that he had tinkered as early as *Soldiers' Pay* with some of the "tools" that later contributed to the presentation of his "heart's darling." The strategy of the "empty center," in fact, can be seen as having its inception in that first novel, where the hopelessly wounded aviator, Donald Mahon, though an infinitely less complex character than Caddy, occupies a corresponding position in the text's narrative structure. Mahon, as Cleanth Brooks puts it, is the "quiet center about which most of the action in the novel revolves." He serves "as the empty eye of the hurricane, itself nothingness, though it is the cause of the powerful forces that swirl around it."[37] Although, unlike Caddy, Mahon is physically (if not mentally) on the scene for most of the action and is not primarily characterized through the distorted lens of private memory, he too functions as a symbol of loss and elicits a similarly broad range of personal responses from those who are associated with him. Just as Caddy is seen by the various members of her family as "sister and mother, virgin and whore, angel and demon,"[38] so Mahon is viewed alternately as hero and casualty, son and lover, faun and shade by those who surround him. By the end of each novel, however, all of these images resolve into the vanishing point of pain and absence: the loving sister ultimately cannot return; the fading shadow of a soldier must receive his final pay.

It is possible that Faulkner's conception and initial development of this narrative strategy was directly influenced by one of his favorite works of fiction, Joseph Conrad's *The Nigger of the "Narcissus."*[39] In the introduction to the American edition of 1914, with which (or with one of its reprints) Faulkner was most probably familiar, Conrad himself explicitly discusses his novel's underlying structure, one that has particular relevance for the kind of circular design that Faulkner first experimented with in *Soldiers' Pay*. Even though *The Nigger of the "Narcissus"* was "written round" the dying sailor James Wait, Conrad declared, "he is nothing; he is merely the centre of the ship's collective psychology and the pivot of the action."[40] The dying Mahon, when compared to a conventionally drawn fictional character, is likewise "nothing"; blind, maimed, and practically comatose, he often seems little more than a narrative prop. He functions, indeed, as precisely the kind of pivotal symbol Conrad describes.

Whether or not Faulkner actually derived it from Conrad, it is clear that this strategy, developed and refined in *Flags in the Dust* as well as in *Soldiers' Pay*, had, by the time he completed *The Sound and the Fury*, become a significant and characteristic feature of his narrative art. The pivotal

figure around which *Flags in the Dust* revolves is John
Sartoris, Bayard's reckless but lovable brother and the secret
object of Narcissa's affection. Although he is displayed
somewhat less prominently than Mahon or Caddy, he occupies a similar structural position and fulfills a similar narrative function. Since he dies in aerial combat almost a year
before *Flags in the Dust* opens, he never appears in the
narrative present, but is portrayed—unlike Mahon but clearly
anticipating Caddy—entirely in terms of other characters'
memories of him. Along with Narcissa and Bayard, Aunt
Jenny, Aunt Sally, Caspey, the MacCallums, and even Frankie
provide glimpses of him, so that, like the absent Caddy, his
ghostly presence pervades the narrative.

However, the similarity in technique between these novels is directly related to larger similarities of narrative preoccupation. In each case, the actions of the centripetal figures
reverberate through time. They themselves, however, are
beyond time; they can only be interpreted, never under-
stood. Their various meanings for the remaining characters
and for the reader can never be stabilized, but must, in
Jacques Derrida's terms, forever circle around a point of
absence.[41] Original presence is irrecoverable and relationships can be approached only by the force of desire.[42] Just
as John's loss creates a void that the survivors vainly attempt
to fill—Bayard by obsessively trying to duplicate his foolhardy death and Narcissa by attaching herself to Bayard, a
debased copy of her original love[43]—so Caddy's absence
creates an unbridgeable gap in the emotional life of her
family, leading to essentially the same kind of desperate and
self-destructive consequences.[44] John and Bayard's un-
usually strong fraternal bond, moreover, distinctly prefigures Benjy and Quentin's abnormally intense attachment to
their sister, and the pain and disruption precipitated by John's
death similarly anticipates the suffering and disillusion caused
by the loss of Caddy.

Faulkner, in fact, reread his previous work for many central aspects of the Compsons' family life. In particular, the psychologically complex connection between lack of parental love and brother-sister incest had occupied Faulkner from the very outset of his career. Even a cursory survey of the early fiction reveals that the "normal" or traditional family, consisting of two parental figures—the love-dispensing mother and authoritarian father—is for Faulkner the exception rather than the rule. Mothers are literally absent (dead or missing) from the Mahon family in *Soldiers' Pay*, the Robyn family in *Mosquitoes*, and the Sartoris and Benbow families in *Flags in the Dust*, and they are symbolically absent (emotionally and morally ineffectual) from the Hodge family in "Elmer."[45] With the exception of Mahon (who is an only child), absent or inadequate maternal love is in each of these cases directly associated with an intensified and potentially dangerous sibling attachment. The twins, Bayard and John, thus form what amounts to a pathological bond (at least for Bayard, the survivor), while the brother-sister pairs—Josh and Patricia (also twins), Elmer and Jo-Addie, Horace and Narcissa—seek compensatory love in the "forbidden game" of incest.[46]

The Compson family thus fits a configuration already characteristic of Faulkner's work.[47] Although the nominal matriarch, Caroline Compson, outwardly pays lip service to her maternal role—"But it's my place to suffer for my children" (*SF*, p. 274)—she remains a cold, egocentric and totally negative figure unable to rise above narcissistic hypochondria, petty social concerns, and an abstract and repressive morality, even though they effectively destroy her relationship with her children. Jason Compson III, the nominal patriarch, emerges as a fundamentally weak and defeated man, whose natural love, idealism, and compassion have been progressively worn away by the burden of a constantly whining and loveless wife, to be replaced only by a kind of cynical acceptance of things as they are. Rather than provide the advice and authority his children so urgently need, he takes solace in nihilistic philosophy and the contents of the "sideboard," finally succumbing to alcoholic passivity and death. Both parents, in short, are effectively absent, and the Compson children not only experience what Faulkner later called "the tragic complexity of . . . motherless childhood"[48] (Quentin, as neurotic spokesman, repeatedly cries "if I'd just had a mother" [for example, *SF*, p. 213]), they also suffer from the lack of a proper father.[49] In this respect, Quentin's symbolic image of his parents is brutally apt: "there was a picture in one of our books, a dark place into which a single weak ray of light came slanting upon two faces lifted out of the shadow. . . . I'd have to turn back to it until the dungeon was Mother herself she and Father upward into weak light holding hands and us lost somewhere below even them without even a ray of light" (*SF*, p. 215). Here, the Compson children remain forever below, in the dark void of lovelessness ("without even a ray of light"), while the imprisoning mother restrains the would-be compassionate but now ineffectual father. Although in the early portion of the novel Mr. Compson is glimpsed as providing some of the sympathy and affection that his wife so obviously lacks, it is the loving sister Caddy who, at least temporarily, fills the maternal gap.[50] It is entirely consistent with the pattern established in the earlier novels that she should become the object of her motherless brothers' incestuous desires.[51]

Faulkner thus once again returns to his past; but, as always, it is a return with a difference. Whereas in the earlier fiction he explored only the incestuous consequences of maternal absence, in *The Sound and the Fury* he places the motherless family right at the novel's core and dramatizes the Compsons' deterioration and downfall specifically in terms of the social and psychological damage resulting from such a lack. By presenting a detailed picture of the loveless mother and the lost sister, Faulkner ensures that the maternal void remains unfilled and thus forcibly emphasizes the Compsons' irremediable loss.

Faulkner's capacity to reuse previous materials and techniques in radically altered—and profoundly enriched—ways is especially evident at the very end of *The Sound and the Fury*, which distinctly draws on the ending of *Soldiers' Pay*. In noting that the conclusions of both novels rely on the evocation of a black religious service, critics have said little about more detailed and significant correspondences, such as the physical resemblance between the two houses of worship, their analogous geographical settings, and the similar manner in which they are depicted.[52] Both the "shabby church" in *Soldiers' Pay* (*SP*, p. 319) and the "weathered church" in *The Sound and the Fury* (*SF*, p. 364) are situated among groves of trees beside dirt roads and have curious architectural appendages: the former displays a "canting travesty of a spire"; the latter, a "crazy steeple." Both, moreover, are described in pictorial terms and appear as flat, two-dimensional scenes, entirely "without perspective." There are other correspondences between the endings: the two final chapters open in kitchens where, in both instances, there "was no sound save a clock" (*SP*, p. 296; cf. *SF*, p. 355). At the Mahons', the ticking becomes portentously symbolic: "The clock went Life. Death. Life. Death" (*SP*, p. 297). At the Compsons', the "clock tick-tocked, solemn and profound. It might have been the dry pulse of the decaying house itself" (*SF*, p. 355). Furthermore, the dénouement of both novels is prefaced by sinister bird cries— "hellish" jaybirds in *The Sound and the Fury* (*SF*, pp. 331, 335) and "dusty" sparrows in *Soldiers' Pay* (*SP*, pp. 296–97)—and culminates in very much the same kind of "wordless" apotheosis (*SP*, p. 318; *SF*, p. 367).

What is more to the point here, however, is the way in

which Faulkner narratively assimilated and imaginatively
transmuted these rereadings of his past. Whereas in *Soldiers' Pay* he depicted the affirmative, visionary quality of
the climactic black service in purely abstract terms, evoking
the "Oneness with Something, somewhere" (*SP*, p. 319)
solely through reference to the overheard voices that had
"become beautiful with mellow longing, passionate and sad"
(*SP*, p. 319), in *The Sound and the Fury* he epitomizes and
gives substance to such transcendent voices in the masterful
dramatization of the Reverend Shegog's sermon. At the end
of *Soldiers' Pay*, the narrator attempted to describe the
"crooning submerged passion of the dark race" (*SP*, p. 319)
as it was experienced from the outside, discursively explaining: "It was nothing, it was everything; then it swelled to
an ecstasy, taking the white man's words as readily as it
took his remote God and made a personal Father of Him"
(*SP*, p. 319). In *The Sound and the Fury*, the narrator takes
the reader right into the church and presents the transfiguration itself, focusing directly on the stages by which the
Easter service is metamorphosed into a heightened celebration of spiritual communion.[53] Faulkner not only supplies
Shegog's powerful words, he details the process by which
the monkeylike man becomes the sacred vessel and servant
of the Word,[54] charting his crucial shift from the cold "virtuosity" of the white man's language to the incantatory emotionalism of black speech, with its "sad, timbrous quality
like an alto horn," and finally calling attention to the way in
which "the voice consumed him, until he was nothing and
[the congregation was] nothing and there was not even a
voice but instead their hearts were speaking to one another
in chanting measures beyond the need for words" (*SF*,
p. 367).

This climactic moment of exaltation and release constitutes, of course, only one element of the novel's elaborately
orchestrated resolution.[55] While Dilsey is participating in

the Easter ritual, "crying rigidly and quietly in the anneal-ment and the blood of the remembered Lamb" (*SF*, p. 371), Jason is off on a futile quest of violence and revenge, con-cerned more with "dragging Omnipotence down from His throne" (*SF*, p. 382) than with commemorating the return of the resurrected son to His right hand. That Faulkner should at the novel's conclusion counterpoint the quiet fulfillment of Dilsey's religious experience with Jason's furious journey of hate and destruction is, of course, entirely consistent with the positive/negative patterns that had earlier informed the endings of *Soldiers' Pay* and *Flags in the Dust*. It is no less important that he makes these antithetical actions overlap each other in time, insisting by a system of subtle yet per-sistent cross-references that the reader perceive them as oc-curring simultaneously.[56] Like the parallel presentation of the black choir and "the facts of division and death" in *Soldiers' Pay* (*SP*, pp. 318–19), or of Benbow Sartoris's birth and young Bayard's death in *Flags in the Dust*, the concurrence of the Easter celebration and Jason's disastrous search for Quentin at the conclusion of *The Sound and the Fury* provides a dual focus on the alternative and contrasting perspectives; it thus ensures that the religious affirmation (like the repeated sound of the church bells) reverberates throughout the final movement toward breakdown and de-spair, mitigating what would otherwise be a totally negative resolution.

The final scene at the monument symbolically reiterates both terms of this suspension: loss and destruction find expression in Jason's unleashed violence and in the horrific cry of "tongueless" agony, and the culminating evocation of Benjy's "blue and serene" eyes specifically recalls his "sweet blue gaze" at the climax of the Reverend Shegog's sermon. The closing evocation of temporarily restored balance and control—"as cornice and façade flowed smoothly once more from left to right; post and tree, window and doorway, and signboard, each in its ordered place" (*SF*, p. 401)—arrests rather than resolves the novel's major tensions by invoking natural images of quietude and cessation, which insist in themselves that a conclusion of some kind has been reached. There is characteristically no dramatic fulfillment or terminal action that would allow us to "retrospectively pattern" preceding details and achieve some kind of final and exhaustive alignment.[57] Our formal sense of completion is satisfied by the language itself. Faulkner arrives at what James calls a novel's "visibly-appointed stopping place" not only by foregrounding "closural allusions" ("serene," "empty," "ordered"),[58] but also by placing them within a climactic rhetorical structure that builds the individual elements ("post," "tree") into a stable and harmonious whole. Here, just as in his previous fiction—in the rhetorical finale of *Flags in the Dust*, in the measured cadences of the concluding sentences of *Soldiers' Pay*, or even as far back as in the poetic terminations of "Frankie and Johnny" and "Peter"—Faulkner breaks off rather than works out his conclusions, providing the force of closure through linguistic means rather than through a rounding out of narrative or thematic patterns. In this respect, then, even the ending of *The Sound and the Fury* can be said to involve a return to Faulkner's beginnings.

To emphasize the indebtedness of *The Sound and the Fury* to Faulkner's earlier exercises in fiction is not of course to suggest that these are the only ghostly presences in the text—the only works he had learned to read creatively.[59] There has been, in particular, much discussion of Joyce's influence, especially with regard to narrative strategy, and it is undoubtedly true that *The Sound and the Fury* could not have been written in the form in which it exists without a knowledge, however fragmentary, of Joyce's work and a clear sense of its ambitious scope and its technical limitations.[60] It can, in fact, be argued that Faulkner's use of stream of consciousness in *The Sound and the Fury*, especially in the radically innovative opening section, with its unprecedented temporal dislocations and linguistic denudations, represents a deliberate attempt on the part of the younger novelist to push the technique forward beyond the point that Joyce had reached in, say, the Proteus episode of *Ulysses*. It is also possible to see his characteristic use of initially disconcerting thematic preludes as constituting a similar attempt to move beyond the fragmented overture that opened the Sirens episode. There seems no point in rehearsing the demonstrable correspondences between *The Sound and the Fury* and Joyce's work, except to say that they are entirely consistent with Faulkner's characteristic practice of learning what he could from his most adventurous predecessors and contemporaries, and that his reading of Joyce and other novelists undoubtedly contributed, directly or indirectly, to those creative processes by which *The Sound and the Fury* came into being.

During his apprenticeship Faulkner not only progressively changed his "masters," moving from duplications of Swinburne and Eliot through a host of minor and ultimately uncongenial models—such as Cabell and Huxley—to a new awareness of the potentialities of such commanding figures as Conrad and Joyce, but he also changed his fundamental attitude toward them. As Willard Huntington Wright had argued, "No one can commence building an art where his most advanced predecessor left off. He must travel the same road as that taken by his predecessor if he is to outdistance him."[61] By the time Faulkner reached *The Sound and the Fury*, he had learned that this road not only involved the imitation and assimilation of the expressive conventions of his craft, but also a belief in the possibility, or perhaps even the necessity, of furthering that craft, outdistancing his masters by the exploitation of purely private resources—resources that he learned to develop by reading himself. With this text, as Faulkner wrote in a 1933 draft introduction, he became aware of the personal consequences of his reading, discovering, as if for the first time, "the Flauberts and Dostoievskys and Conrads," that he had "consumed whole" years before.[62] He also, and more importantly for his future career, realized the necessity of confronting form anew; having taught himself to read his predecessors through this experience of trying to match and then surpass them, just as he had taught himself to read his own past, it was now time to "quit reading," secure in the assurance that his artistic self had been found.[63]

In *The Sound and the Fury* Faulkner first drew on the full range of received conventions, as well as on the full range of his innovative genius, and thus passed through what Wright had called that "hazardous period" of apprenticeship to enter finally on his "individual destiny." While writing *The Sound and the Fury*, Faulkner was as ready to draw on his own reading and literary past as he had been in writing his apprentice works, but he now did so with a greatly increased awareness, self-assurance, and sense of aesthetic freedom—based precisely on the wide experience he had already gained, on the belief that there was, especially in *Soldiers' Pay* and *Flags in the Dust*, work of his own worth borrowing from, and on the new sense of himself as belonging in the company of such masters of his craft as James, Conrad, Flaubert, Dostoyevsky, and Turgenev and as needing to acknowledge no limitations other than those of his own energy, talent, and humanity.[64]

What is crucial here is that in *The Sound and the Fury*— as distinct from all of his previous work—Faulkner's imaginative assimilation of his "sources," as of his self-borrowings, constitutes an absolute transformation rather than a mere transfer. It is as if the old dialectic between dependence and independence had been resolved in terms of the discovery of an active and retroactive self-dependence. The fragmented structure, characterized by the juxtaposition of linguistically distinct formal units which had informed so many of his early productions, is now merged with his previous experiments in point of view to produce a radically new and infinitely more dramatic combination: each textually bounded section has its own language, temporal dimension, and narrative perspective. The vagrant voices that floated through *Soldiers' Pay* and *Mosquitoes* are now specified and given flesh, firmly positioned in time, space, and idiom. The discursively fecund world of *Flags in the Dust* is now made functional, articulated in voice—most notably in the Jason section—as well as in highly particularized representations of place. And the protean search for expressive diversity and flexibility is now located at the very center of the text's structural principles.

In *The Sound and the Fury*, motivated by whatever personal impulses, feeling that he need be under no imaginative restraints, and writing only for himself, Faulkner was able for the first time to marshal all his resources. Taking possession of the territory that he had so carefully mapped in *Flags in the Dust*, adapting the narrative structures he had devised in "Elmer" and *Soldiers' Pay*, and harking back to the organizational procedures of *The Marble Faun*, he thus arrived at a cumulative and totally transformed synthesis of those aspects of his genius for which he had previously found only brief and fragmentary expression. In the process of composing *The Sound and the Fury*, as he later acknowledged, Faulkner at last succeeded in setting in motion "that part of me which learned as I wrote, which perhaps is the very force which drives a writer to the travail of invention and the drudgery of putting seventy-five or a hundred thousand words on paper."[65]

Notes

1. The Will to Create: Poetry and Imitation

1. André Bleikasten, *The Most Splendid Failure: Faulkner's "The Sound and the Fury"* (Bloomington: Indiana University Press, 1976); "Faulkner before Faulkner" is the title of the chapter that deals with Faulkner's work up to *The Sound and the Fury*.

2. Michel Foucault, "What Is an Author?" trans. Josué V. Harari, in *Textual Strategies: Perspectives in Poststructural Criticism*, ed. Josué V. Harari (Ithaca: Cornell University Press, 1979), pp. 141–60.

3. Bleikasten, *Splendid Failure*, p. 5. On the general pattern of Faulkner's career, also see Gary Lee Stonum, *Faulkner's Career: An Internal Literary History* (Ithaca: Cornell University Press, 1979), pp. 13–40.

4. Bleikasten, *Splendid Failure*, p. 5.

5. In *The Life of the Poet: Beginning and Ending Poetic Careers* (Chicago: University of Chicago Press, 1981), Lawrence Lipking sees such "initiation" as the crucial first stage in a poet's career. See especially pp. 15–16, 20.

6. Bleikasten, *Splendid Failure*, p. 5.

7. Thomas McFarland, "The Originality Paradox," *New Literary History* 5 (1974): 447–76.

8. In the *Anatomy of Criticism* (Princeton: Princeton University Press, 1957), p. 97, Northrop Frye offers perhaps the most concise description of the inherent intertextuality of literature: "Poetry can only be made out of other poems; novels out of other novels."

9. In *The Burden of the Past and the English Poet* (Cambridge: Harvard University Press, 1970), pp. 3–4, W. Jackson Bate quotes an Egyptian scribe of 2000 B.C.: "Would I had phrases that are not known, utterances that are strange, in a new language that has not been used, free from repetition, not an utterance which has grown stale, which men of old have spoken." For other discussions of the originality paradox, see, for example, in addition to McFarland and Bate, Harold Bloom, *The Anxiety of Influence: A Theory of Poetry* (London: Oxford Univer-

sity Press, 1973); Loy D. Martin, "Literary Invention: The Illusion of the Individual Talent," *Critical Inquiry* 6 (1980): 649–67; K. K. Ruthven, *Critical Assumptions* (Cambridge: Cambridge University Press, 1979), pp. 102–34; Claudio Guillén, *Literature as System: Essays toward the Theory of Literary History* (Princeton: Princeton University Press, 1971), pp. 17–68; and Harold Ogden White, *Plagiarism and Imitation during the English Renaissance* (Cambridge: Harvard University Press, 1935).

10. Bloom, *The Anxiety of Influence*, and, to a lesser extent, Bate, *The Burden of the Past*, see the paradox ultimately experienced as an anxiety; Martin, "Literary Invention," pp. 666–67, sees it experienced as a tension.

11. Longinus, *On the Sublime*, trans. W. Rhys Roberts (Cambridge: Cambridge University Press, 1935), p. 81.

12. See, for example, George P. Garrett, Jr., "An Examination of the Poetry of William Faulkner," *Princeton University Library Chronicle* 18 (1957): 124–35; Cleanth Brooks, *William Faulkner: Toward Yoknapatawpha and Beyond* (New Haven: Yale University Press, 1978), pp. 1–31, 346–51; Joseph Blotner, *Faulkner: A Biography*, 2 vols. (New York: Random House, 1974), vol. 1, chaps. 14–21 passim; Richard P. Adams, *Faulkner: Myth and Motion* (Princeton: Princeton University Press, 1968), pp. 16–25; H. Edward Richardson, *William Faulkner: The Journey to Self-Discovery* (Columbia: University of Missouri Press, 1969), pp. 46–85, 107–15, 213–16; Margaret Yonce, "Faulkner's 'Atthis' and 'Attis': Some Sources of Myth," *Mississippi Quarterly* 23 (1970): 289–98; Egbert William Oldenburg, "William Faulkner's Early Experiments with Narrative Techniques" (Ph.D. diss., University of Michigan, 1966), pp. 30–51; Martin Kreiswirth, "Faulkner as Translator: His Versions of Verlaine," *Mississippi Quarterly* 30 (1977): 429–32; and Martin Kreiswirth, "Faulkner's *The Marble Faun*: Dependence and Independence," *English Studies in Canada* 6 (1980): 333–44.

13. Quoted in Emily Whitehurst Stone, "How a Writer Finds His Materials," *Harper's*, Nov. 1965, p. 158.

14. "Letter from Phil Stone to Louis Cochran," 28 Dec. 1931, in James B. Meriwether, "Early Notices of Faulkner by Phil Stone and Louis Cochran," *Mississippi Quarterly* 17 (1964): 141.

15. See Martin Kreiswirth, "The Will to Create: Faulkner's Apprenticeship and Willard Huntington Wright," *Arizona Quarterly* 37 (1981): 149–65.

16. See Frances Blazer O'Brien, "Faulkner and Wright, Alias S. S. Van Dine," *Mississippi Quarterly* 14 (1961): 101–7; M. Gidley, "Wil-

liam Faulkner and Willard Huntington Wright's *The Creative Will*," *Canadian Review of American Studies* 9 (1978): 169–77; Blotner, *Faulkner*, 1:320–22.

17. Willard Huntington Wright, *The Creative Will: Studies in the Philosophy and the Syntax of Aesthetics* (New York: John Lane, 1916), p. 225; the preceding quotations in this paragraph appear respectively on pp. 181, 193, 77, 195, 182–83.

18. See Brooks, *Toward Yoknapatawpha*, p. 3; and Blotner, *Faulkner*, 1:184–85, *40*. Also see Carvel Collins, "Biographical Background for Faulkner's *Helen*," in William Faulkner, *Helen: A Courtship and Mississippi Poems* (New Orleans: Tulane University Press; Oxford, Miss.: Yoknapatawpha Press, 1981), pp. 48–49, 66.

19. See, for example, Richard P. Adams, "The Apprenticeship of William Faulkner," *Tulane Studies in English* 12 (1962): 120. Of course, the distinction between plagiarism and imitation has not been easy to formulate; see McFarland, "The Originality Paradox," pp. 469–76.

20. The typescript is described in Keen Butterworth, "A Census of Manuscripts and Typescripts of William Faulkner's Poetry," *Mississippi Quarterly* 26 (1973): item 28, p. 341. Swinburne's poem is in *The Complete Works of Algernon Charles Swinburne*, ed. Edmund Gosse and Thomas J. Wise, 20 vols. (London: Heinemann, 1925), 1:212.

21. Swinburne, *Complete Works*, 1:212.

22. Faulkner employs similar Elizabethan diction in Poems XVI, XXI, and XL of *A Green Bough*.

23. In Poems XXIV and XL of *A Green Bough*, which deal with the same subject matter, Faulkner can be seen as directly experimenting with the different effects produced by Victorian and Elizabethan models. Also see Faulkner, *Helen: A Courtship*, Poem X, p. 121.

24. For some psychobiographical speculations with regard to this poem, see John Irwin, *Doubling and Incest/Repetition and Revenge: A Speculative Reading of Faulkner* (Baltimore: Johns Hopkins University Press, 1975), pp. 164–68.

25. See Brooks, *Toward Yoknapatawpha*, pp. 8–9, 346–47, 373–74. Also see Collins, "Background for *Helen*," pp. 45–46, 88.

26. See Cleanth Brooks, "Faulkner as Poet," *Southern Literary Journal* 1 (1968): 9–11.

27. Although some fragments of individual poems of *Vision in Spring* exist in the Humanities Research Center, University of Texas, the complete typescript is in the Faulkner Collection, Alderman Library, University of Virginia. Some of the poems, or revised versions of them, were subsequently published; see Poems II, V, XX (*GB*, 12–15, 22–23,

42); "Portrait," *The Double Dealer* 3 (1922): 337 (reprinted in *EP*, pp. 99–100); "Nocturne," *Ole Miss, 1920–21* (University, Miss., 1921), pp. 214–15 (reprinted in *EP*, pp. [82]–[83]); and "Visions in Spring" and "April," *Contempo* 1 (Feb. 1, 1932): 1, 2; also see Blotner, *Faulkner*, 1:307–12. Astonishing as it may seem, the evidence suggests that Faulkner did not intend these weak imitations of Eliot to be parodic or ironic; Eliot's techniques are flatly duplicated, not exaggerated or undercut.

28. There has been much speculation concerning Eliot's influence on Faulkner. The most useful studies are Adams, "Apprenticeship," pp. 116–18; Blotner, *Faulkner*, 1:307–10; Brooks, *Toward Yoknapatawpha*, pp. 11–16, 29–30, 78–81, 347–49; and Frederick L. Gwynn, "Faulkner's Prufrock—and Other Observations," *Journal of English and Germanic Philology* 52 (1953): 63–70. Also see Ida Fasel, "A 'Conversation' between Faulkner and Eliot," *Mississippi Quarterly* 20 (1967): 195–206; Mary E. McGann, "*The Waste Land* and *The Sound and the Fury*: To Apprehend the Human Process Moving in Time," *Southern Literary Journal* 9 (1976): 13–21; and Diane Naples, "Eliot's 'Tradition' and *The Sound and the Fury*," *Modern Fiction Studies* 20 (1974): 214–17.

29. Blotner, *Faulkner*, 1:309; also see Butterworth, "A Census of Faulkner's Poetry," item 28, p. 353.

30. See Butterworth, "A Census of Faulkner's Poetry," item 36, pp. 342–43. Also see Joan St. C. Crane and Anne E. H. Freudenberg, comps., *Man Collecting: Manuscripts and Printed Works of William Faulkner in the University of Virginia Library* (Charlottesville: University of Virginia Printing Office, 1975), pp. 20–23; and Robert Hamblin and Louis Daniel Brodsky, *Selections from the William Faulkner Collection of Louis Daniel Brodsky: A Descriptive Catalogue* (Charlottesville: University Press of Virginia, 1979), pp. 28, 30, 31–32.

31. Faulkner altered the pronouns several times in different versions of the poem. See Crane and Freudenberg, *Man Collecting*, pp. 21–23; and Hamblin and Brodsky, *Selections from the Faulkner Collection*, p. 30. Also see Margaret Yonce, "'Shot Down Last Spring': The Wounded Aviators of Faulkner's Wasteland," *Mississippi Quarterly* 31 (1978): 359–68; and Oldenburg, "Faulkner's Early Experiments," pp. 40–46.

32. See Kreiswirth, "Faulkner as Translator," pp. 430–32.

33. See Kreiswirth, "Faulkner's *The Marble Faun*," pp. 333–43.

34. See François Pitavy, "Faulkner poète," *Études anglaises* 29 (1976): 456–67; and Brooks, "Faulkner as Poet," pp. 13–19.

35. Bleikasten, *Splendid Failure*, p. 7.

36. Wright, *The Creative Will*, p. 207.

2. The Curse of Tongues: Apprenticeship in Prose

1. See Austin McGiffert Wright, *The American Short Story in the Twenties* (Chicago: University of Chicago Press, 1961), especially chap. 11, for a discussion of the popular "short story" as distinguished from the freer, more deliberately artistic "episode" that was gaining wider recognition at this time.

2. "The Hill" has received considerable critical attention. See, for example, Michel Gresset, "Faulkner's 'The Hill,'" *Southern Literary Journal* 6 (1974): 3–18; Philip Momberger, "A Reading of Faulkner's 'The Hill,'" *Southern Literary Journal* 9 (1977): 16–29; Cleanth Brooks, *William Faulkner: Toward Yoknapatawpha and Beyond* (New Haven: Yale University Press, 1978), pp. 39–41, 46–47; Richard P. Adams, *Faulkner: Myth and Motion* (Princeton: Princeton University Press, 1968), pp. 23–27; André Bleikasten, *The Most Splendid Failure: Faulkner's "The Sound and the Fury"* (Bloomington: Indiana University Press, 1976), pp. 11–14; H. Edward Richardson, *William Faulkner: The Journey to Self-Discovery* (Columbia: University of Missouri Press, 1969), pp. 99–103; and Hans H. Skei, "The Novelist as Short Story Writer" (Ph.D. diss., University of Oslo, 1980), pp. 208–14.

3. William Faulkner, "Nympholepsy," ed. James B. Meriwether, *Mississippi Quarterly* 26 (1973): 403–9; reprinted in, William Faulkner, *Uncollected Stories*, ed. Joseph Blotner (New York: Random House, 1979), pp. 331–37.

4. In *Toward Yoknapatawpha*, pp. 363–64, Brooks suggests that Faulkner may have picked up this unusual title from Conrad Aiken's *The Charnel Rose*, even though the term *nympholepsy* is "never mentioned in the poem itself." Aiken, however, uses the word in the preface to *The Charnel Rose*, in *The Charnel Rose, Senlin: A Biography, and Other Poems* (Boston: Four Seas, 1918). He defines it in a way that has relevance for Faulkner's story: the theme of the poem "might be called nympholepsy—nympholepsy as that impulse which sends us from one dream, or ideal, to another, always disillusioned, always creating for adoration some new and subtler fiction" (p. 91). As Carvel Collins points out, Faulkner's use of the word might also owe something to his reading of George Moore's *Memoirs of My Dead Life* (1906) ("Biographical Background for Faulkner's *Helen*," in William Faulkner, *Helen: A Courtship and Mississippi Poems* [New Orleans: Tulane University Press; Oxford, Miss.: Yoknapatawpha Press, 1981], pp. 51–52).

5. Faulkner's commedia dell'arte figures appear, for example, in "Fantoches" (*EP*, p. 57), and "Nocturne" (*EP*, pp. [82]–[83]), and the

unpublished "The World of Pierrot: A Nocturne," partly quoted in Joseph Blotner, *Faulkner: A Biography*, 2 vols. (New York: Random House, 1974), 1:307–8. For the "Shade of Pierrot," see William Faulkner, *The Marionettes* (Charlottesville: University Press of Virginia, 1977), pp. 2–3. It is perhaps worth pointing out that in manuscript *The Sound and the Fury* was originally entitled "Twilight."

6. "Twilight" first appeard in *Contempo* 1 (Feb. 1, 1932): 1, a little magazine published in Chapel Hill, and subsequently as Poem X of *GB*; typescript evidence does not indicate its date of composition, so it is impossible to determine its precise relationship to "The Hill"; see Keen Butterworth, "A Census of Manuscripts and Typescripts of William Faulkner's Poetry," *Mississippi Quarterly* 26 (1973): item 68, p. 349. Also see Adams, *Myth and Motion*, pp. 22–23; and Brooks, *Toward Yoknapatawpha*, pp. 46–47.

7. *The Complete Works of Algernon Charles Swinburne*, ed. Edmund Gosse and Thomas J. Wise, 20 vols. (London: Heinemann, 1925), 1:334.

8. For a discussion of Faulkner's use of negative structures in the mature fiction, see J. E. Bunselmeyer, "Faulkner's Narrative Styles," *American Literature* 53 (1981): 420–42, especially 425–30.

9. Willard Huntington Wright, *The Creative Will: Studies in the Philosophy and the Syntax of Aesthetics* (New York: John Lane, 1916), pp. 153–54.

10. William Faulkner, "Review of *Ducdame*," ed. James B. Meriwether, *Mississippi Quarterly* 28 (1975): 343.

11. Wright, *The Creative Will*, p. 154.

12. Ibid., p. 153.

13. See Philip Momberger, "A Critical Study of Faulkner's Early Sketches and Collected Stories" (Ph.D. diss., Johns Hopkins, 1970), pp. 66–71; Leland Cox, "Sinbad in New Orleans: Early Short Fiction by William Faulkner—An Annotated Edition" (Ph.D. diss., University of South Carolina, 1977), pp. lvii–lxvii; Cleanth Brooks, "A Note on Faulkner's Early Attempts at the Short Story," *Studies in Short Fiction* 10 (1973): 382–83; and Skei, "The Novelist as Short Story Writer," pp. 237–39, 250–51.

14. Cf. Théophile Gautier, *Mademoiselle de Maupin* (New York: Boni and Liveright, n.d.), p. 133: "Three things please me: gold, marble, and purple, splendour, solidity, and colour." Faulkner owned this edition; see Joseph Blotner, comp., *William Faulkner's Library: A Catalogue* (Charlottesville: University Press of Virginia, 1964), p. 94; also see Michael Millgate, *The Achievement of William Faulkner* (London: Constable,

1966), p. 300. Compare Faulkner's nautical opening, "The Waves of Destiny . . ." with the opening of Conrad's *Heart of Darkness*, according to Faulkner one of the "best stories he had ever read" (*NO*, p. xviii).

15. "Song Number Two" appeared in *The Double Dealer* 7 (Nov.–Dec. 1924): 59–60, and "Song Number One," in the previous issue, 7 (Oct. 1924): 15.

16. Swinburne, *Complete Works*, 1:234–35.

17. See Michael Millgate, "Starting Out in the Twenties: Reflections on *Soldiers' Pay*," *Mosaic* 7 (1973): 5.

18. Hearn's sketch is quoted in John S. Kendall, "Lafcadio Hearn in New Orleans: I. On the Item," *The Double Dealer* 3 (May 1922): 237; the second part of the article, "II. On the Times-Democrat," *The Double Dealer* 3 (June 1922): 313–23, appeared in the same issue that contained Faulkner's poem "Portrait."

19. A further example of this technical diversity appears in "Hong Li," which was added to the other monologues of "New Orleans" when Faulkner collected them for Estelle Oldham in a handmade pamphlet in late 1926. This piece was first printed in Noel Polk, "'Hong Li' and *Royal Street*: The New Orleans Sketches in Manuscript," *Mississippi Quarterly* 26 (1973): 394–95. For a facsimile reproduction of the sketch, see Noel Polk, "William Faulkner's 'Hong Li' on *Royal Street*," *Library Chronicle of the University of Texas at Austin*, n.s., 13 (1980): 27–30.

20. Wright, *The Creative Will*, pp. 141, 186.

21. William Faulkner, *Helen: A Courtship*, p. 112.

22. William Faulkner, "The Priest," ed. James B. Meriwether, *Mississippi Quarterly* 29 (1976): 445–50; reprinted in, Faulkner, *Uncollected Stories*, pp. 348–51. Also see Cox, "Sinbad in New Orleans," p. lxx.

23. The order in which "New Orleans" and "The Cobbler" were published suggests, of course, that for these pieces this may indeed be the case.

24. Faulkner, "The Priest," p. 449, 450. Barthes's codes may help to clarify these distinctions. Whereas the two versions of each sketch are built of semic, symbolic, referential, and hermeneutic elements, the longer texts depend on proairetic elements—the sequences of represented actions and the reader's construction of them—to a much greater extent than the "New Orleans" versions. The proairetic code, in fact, is virtually absent from the shorter version of "The Priest." See Roland Barthes, *S/Z*, trans. Richard Miller (New York: Hill and Wang, 1974), pp. 17–30.

25. Faulkner, "The Priest," p. 446. For echoes of F. Scott Fitzgerald in this passage, see Gail Moore Morrison, "Faulkner's Priests and Fitzgerald's 'Absolution,'" *Mississippi Quarterly* 32 (1979): 461–63.

26. Gérard Genette, *Narrative Discourse: An Essay in Method*, trans. Jane E. Lewin (Ithaca: Cornell University Press, 1980), p. 174. For extended discussions of this common but ill-defined technique (also referred to as "style indirect libre" and "narrated monologue"), see Dorrit Cohn, "Narrated Monologue: Definition of a Fictional Style," *Comparative Literature* 18 (1966): 97–112; and Paul Hernadi, "Dual Perspective: Free Indirect Discourse and Related Techniques," *Comparative Literature* 24 (1972): 32–44.

27. For these sketches, see *NO*, pp. 34–40, 61–65, 70–75, respectively.

28. See, for example, *LG*, p. 59. On the question of Faulkner's changing opinion of his worth as a short story writer, see Skei, "The Novelist as Short Story Writer," pp. 3–8.

29. See Austin Wright, *The American Short Story*, chap. 11.

30. Faulkner, *Uncollected Stories*, pp. 490, 489, 493–94.

31. William Faulkner, "Frankie and Johnny," ed. James B. Meriwether, *Mississippi Quarterly* 31 (1978): 453–64; reprinted in, Faulkner, *Uncollected Stories*, pp. 338–47.

32. Faulkner, "Frankie and Johnny," p. 464.

33. Victor Shklovsky, "La Construction de la nouvelle et du roman," trans. Tzvetan Todorov, in *Théorie de la littérature*, ed. Tzvetan Todorov (Paris: Editions du Seuil, 1964), pp. 170–77. On this point, also see Jonathan Culler, *Structuralist Poetics: Structuralism, Linguistics, and the Study of Literature* (Ithaca: Cornell University Press, 1975), pp. 222–23; and Frank Kermode, "Sensing Endings," *Nineteenth-Century Fiction* 33 (1978): 146–47.

34. "Little sister Death" also appears in Faulkner's contemporaneous verse, including an untitled manuscript version of "Knew I Love Once," in the Berg Collection, New York Public Library, as well as in another untitled manuscript in the same collection; see Butterworth, "A Census of Faulkner's Poetry," item 34, p. 342.

35. See "Pantaloon in Black" in *Go Down, Moses* (1942) and the ending of *Pylon* (1935) for Faulkner's later variations on this narrative strategy.

36. The untitled two page typescript fragment is in the Berg Collection, New York Public Library. Faulkner's letters appear as "Al Jackson" in *Uncollected Stories*, pp. 474–79.

37. Untitled typescript fragment, Berg Collection, p. 2.

38. William Faulkner, *Essays, Speeches, and Public Letters*, ed. James B. Meriwether (New York: Random House, 1965), p. 7.

3. Learning a Little about Writing: Faulkner's First Novel

1. Typescripts of Poems XXVII, XXXIII, and XIX (which eventually appeared in *GB*, pp. 49–50, 56, 41) are dated February 26, 1925, March 25, 1925, and April 2, 1925, respectively; "To Helen, Swimming," and Poems I, VI, and VII of *Helen* (*Helen: A Courtship and Mississippi Poems* [New Orleans: Tulane University Press; Oxford, Miss.: Yoknapatawpha Press, 1981], pp. 111, 112, 117, 118) were apparently written in June 1925; "The Faun" was contemporaneously published in *The Double Dealer* 7 (1925): 148; and it is possible that Poem III of *GB* and "A Child Looks from His Window" (which appeared in *Contempo* 2 [1932]: 3) also date from this period. See Joseph Blotner, *Faulkner: A Biography*, 2 vols. (New York: Random House, 1974), 1:297–99, for the dating of these last two poems, and Keen Butterworth, "A Census of Manuscripts and Typescripts of William Faulkner's Poetry," *Mississippi Quarterly* 26 (1973): items 55, 34, 16, 21, 23, pp. 347, 342, 338, 339–40, for descriptions of the typescript versions of some of the others.

2. The prize-winning essay appeared in the New Orleans *Item-Tribune*, April 4, 1925, along with a photograph and short biographical sketch; see Blotner, *Faulkner*, 1:411. Faulkner reviewed John Cowper Powys's *Ducdame* in the *Times-Picayune*, March 22, 1925.

3. See Margaret J. Yonce, "The Composition of *Soldiers' Pay*," *Mississippi Quarterly* 33 (1980): 291–326; Francis J. Bosha, *Faulkner's "Soldiers' Pay": A Bibliographic Study* (Troy, N.Y.: Whitson, 1982), pp. 13–25; Leland Cox, "Sinbad in New Orleans: Early Short Fiction by William Faulkner—An Annotated Edition" (Ph.D. diss., University of South Carolina, 1977), pp. xxii–xxx; and Carvel Collins, "Biographical Background for Faulkner's *Helen*," in Faulkner, *Helen: A Courtship*, pp. 15–18.

4. See Michael Millgate, "Starting Out in the Twenties: Reflections on *Soldiers' Pay*," *Mosaic* 7 (1973): 3–4; and Judith Wittenberg, *Faulkner: The Transfiguration of Biography* (Lincoln: University of Nebraska Press, 1979), pp. 44–47. The route of Lowe's train, via Buffalo and Cincinnati, may also specifically point toward Faulkner's personal experience of military life, since he traveled the same route after being demobilized from Toronto in December 1918 (Blotner, *Faulkner*, 1:231).

5. Millgate, "Starting Out in the Twenties," pp. 3–4; for a discussion

of *Soldiers' Pay* as a war novel, see Stanley Cooperman, *World War I and the American Novel* (Baltimore: Johns Hopkins University Press, 1967), pp. 114, 159–62.

6. In "*Soldiers' Pay*: A Critical Study of William Faulkner's First Novel" (Ph.D. diss., University of South Carolina, 1971), pp. 18–19, Margaret J. Yonce traces the name "Yaphank" to a military review, *Yip, Yip, Yaphank*, written by the then Sergeant Irving Berlin.

7. There are two typescript drafts of the novel: one in the Berg Collection, New York Public Library, and another, apparently later, version in the Faulkner Collection, Alderman Library, University of Virginia. In section 1 of the first chapter of the Virginia typescript, Faulkner systematically deleted Gilligan's name, replacing it with "Yaphank" or personal pronouns.

8. In "The Composition of *Soldiers' Pay*," pp. 300–305, Yonce argues that the first section of chapter 1 of *Soldiers' Pay* was originally drafted as a discrete story.

9. Donald Mahon is closely related to the protagonist of "The Lilacs." See Margaret Yonce, "'Shot Down Last Spring': The Wounded Aviators of Faulkner's Wasteland," *Mississippi Quarterly* 31 (1978): 361–62.

10. See Egbert William Oldenburg, "William Faulkner's Early Experiments with Narrative Techniques" (Ph.D. diss., University of Michigan, 1966), pp. 133–35.

11. For Faulkner's various reworkings of this passage in the typescript drafts, see Yonce, "The Composition of *Soldiers' Pay*," pp. 317–20.

12. See Noel Polk, "Introduction," in Faulkner, *The Marionettes* (Charlottesville: University Press of Virginia, 1977), pp. xv–xvi; and Boyd Davis, "Caddy Compson's Eden," *Mississippi Quarterly* 30 (1977): 383–88.

13. Yonce, "*Soldiers' Pay*," pp. 52–56, 128–30; Philip Castille, "Women and Myth in Faulkner's First Novel," *Tulane Studies in English* 23 (1978): 175–86; Robert M. Slabey, "*Soldiers' Pay*: Faulkner's First Novel," *Revue des langues vivantes* 30 (1964): 234–43; Lewis P. Simpson, "Faulkner and the Legend of the Artist," in *Faulkner: Fifty Years after "The Marble Faun*," ed. George H. Wolfe (University: University of Alabama Press, 1976), pp. 84–86; and Thomas L. McHaney, "The Modernism of *Soldiers' Pay*," *William Faulkner: Material, Studies, and Criticism* 3(1980): 23–25.

14. See Cleanth Brooks, *William Faulkner: Toward Yoknapatawpha and Beyond* (New Haven: Yale University Press, 1978), p. 352.

15. John McClure reviewed *Soldiers' Pay* in the *Times-Picayune*, April

11, 1926; reprinted in, *William Faulkner: The Critical Heritage*, ed. John Bassett (London: Routledge and Kegan Paul, 1975), p. 56.

16. See, for example, Michael Millgate, *The Achievement of William Faulkner* (London: Constable, 1966), pp. 63–64; and Addison C. Bross, "*Soldiers' Pay* and the Art of Aubrey Beardsley," *American Quarterly* 19 (1967): 7–9, 16–19.

17. Aldous Huxley, *Crome Yellow* (London: Chatto and Windus, 1921), p. 9. This book was not in Faulkner's library but was among those ordered by Stone in April 1922 (see Joseph Blotner, comp., *William Faulkner's Library: A Catalogue* [Charlottesville: University Press of Virginia, 1964], p. 125).

18. Cf. Huxley, *Crome Yellow*, p. 300.

19. William Faulkner, "Literature and War," in Michael Millgate, "Faulkner on the Literature of the First World War," *Mississippi Quarterly* 26 (1973): 389.

20. Faulkner, "Literature and War," p. 388; also see p. 389.

21. See Millgate, "Starting Out in the Twenties," pp. 5–7; Blotner, *Faulkner*, 1:429; Slabey, "Faulkner's First Novel," pp. 236–37; Emily Dalgarno, "*Soldiers' Pay* and Virginia Woolf," *Mississippi Quarterly* 29 (1976): 339–46; Oldenburg, "Faulkner's Early Experiments," pp. 118–20, 142–44; and Kenneth William Hepburn, "*Soldiers' Pay* to *The Sound and the Fury*: The Development of the Poetic in the Early Novels of William Faulkner" (Ph.D. diss., University of Washington, 1968), pp. 32–40.

22. Hugh Kenner, "Faulkner and Joyce," in *Faulkner, Modernism, and Film*, ed. Evans Harrington and Ann J. Abadie (Jackson: University Press of Mississippi, 1979), pp. 24–25.

23. See Phyllis Franklin, "The Influence of Joseph Hergesheimer upon *Mosquitoes*," *Mississippi Quarterly* 22 (1969): 207–8, in which Hergesheimer's use of this technique is seen as having prompted similar devices in Faulkner's *Mosquitoes*.

24. "A writer," Faulkner said in a 1955 interview, "will steal from any source. He's so busy stealing and using it that he himself probably never knows where he gets what he uses" (*LG*, p. 128).

25. The typescript in the Berg Collection also contains other experiments with a dramatic format, and in one deleted section voices entitled "He" and "She" discuss general questions of time and mutability. Bosha, in his *Bibliographic Study*, pp. 429–30, transcribes this section. He also, on pp. 516–17, transcribes an analogous section that was deleted from the typescript in the Faulkner Collection, Alderman Library, University of Virginia.

26. William Faulkner, *Uncollected Stories*, ed. Joseph Blotner (New York: Random House, 1979), pp. 459–73.

27. In *"Soldiers' Pay* and the Art of Aubrey Beardsley," p. 17, Bross points out that this episode is distinct from all of the other sexual encounters in the novel, in that the couple is presented nude and there is none of the decadent clothes imagery usually associated with lovemaking in *Soldiers' Pay*.

28. Millgate, "Starting Out in the Twenties," p. 5.

29. Cleanth Brooks, "Faulkner's First Novel," *Southern Review* 6 (1970): 1063–65; Yonce, *"Soldiers' Pay,"* pp. 235–40; and Yonce, "'Shot Down,'" pp. 360–62.

30. See, for example, Yonce, *"Soldiers' Pay,"* pp. 42–43, 58–59, 63–64, 182–85; and Millgate, "Starting Out in the Twenties," pp. 5–7, 12.

31. Faulkner, *Uncollected Stories*, pp. 475–503.

32. These rearrangements are seen in the typescript in the Berg Collection; see Yonce, "The Composition of *Soldiers' Pay*," pp. 293–315.

33. See Martin Kreiswirth, "Faulkner's *The Marble Faun*: Dependence and Independence," *English Studies in Canada* 6 (1980): 338–43.

34. See, for example, Joseph Frank, "Spatial Form in Modern Literature," in his *The Widening Gyre: Crisis and Mastery in Modern Literature* (New Brunswick, N.J.: Rutgers University Press, 1968), pp. 3–62, and his more recent "Spatial Form: An Answer to Critics," *Critical Inquiry* 4 (1977): 231–52.

35. On Cecily's sexuality, see Leslie A. Fiedler, *Love and Death in the American Novel*, rev. ed. (New York: Delta, 1966), p. 321; David Williams, *Faulkner's Women: The Myth and the Muse* (Montreal: McGill-Queens University Press, 1977), pp. 39–40; Castille, "Women and Myth in Faulkner's First Novel," pp. 185–86; and Sally R. Page, *Faulkner's Women: Characterization and Meaning* (Deland, Fla.: Everett/Edwards, 1972), pp. 17–19.

36. The emphasis on water imagery in this scene constitutes a revision in the typescript of the novel in the Berg Collection, Faulkner adding the "If I could only cry" motif in holograph.

37. "Rest in Peace in cast repetition: Our motto is one for every cemetery, a cemetery for everyone throughout the land" (*SP*, p. 297).

38. See Yonce, "The Composition of *Soldiers' Pay*," pp. 320–25.

39. William Faulkner, "An Introduction for *The Sound and the Fury*," ed. James B. Meriwether, *Southern Review* 8 (1972): 708.

40. Willard Huntington Wright, *The Creative Will: Studies in the Philosophy and Syntax of Aesthetics* (New York: John Lane, 1916), p. 154.

4. Variations without Progress: From *Soldiers' Pay* to *Mosquitoes*

1. See Joseph Blotner, *Faulkner: A Biography*, 2 vols. (New York: Random House, 1974), 1:444–46, 451, 453.

2. For the most detailed and significant account of this unpublished text, see Thomas L. McHaney, "The Elmer Papers: Faulkner's Comic Portraits of the Artist," *Mississippi Quarterly* 26 (1973): 281–311; also see Cleanth Brooks, *William Faulkner: Toward Yoknapatawpha and Beyond* (New Haven: Yale University Press, 1978), pp. 115–28; Egbert William Oldenburg, "William Faulkner's Early Experiments with Narrative Techniques" (Ph.D. diss., University of Michigan, 1966), pp. 145–73; and Kenneth William Hepburn, "*Soldiers' Pay* to *The Sound and the Fury*: The Development of the Poetic in the Early Novels of William Faulkner" (Ph.D. diss., University of Washington, 1968), pp. 51–79. As McHaney notes, although the typescripts "Portrait of Elmer Hodge," "Growing Pains," and "A Portrait of Elmer" are included with the "Elmer" typescript in the Faulkner Collection, Alderman Library, University of Virginia (hereafter cited as "Elmer" TS), they are evidently later attempts to recast the abandoned novel in shorter forms. "A Portrait of Elmer" appears in William Faulkner, *Uncollected Stories*, ed. Joseph Blotner (New York: Random House, 1979), pp. 610–41; also see p. 710.

3. James B. Meriwether, *The Literary Career of William Faulkner: A Bibliographical Study* (Columbia: University of South Carolina Press, 1971), p. 81.

4. Though the narrative is incomplete, Faulkner's letter to his mother of September 22, 1925, outlines the novel's action and indicates its satiric tone and ironic conclusion: "Elmer is quite a boy. He is tall and almost handsome and he wants to paint pictures. He gets everything a man could want—money, a European title, marries the girl he wants—and she gives away his paint box. So Elmer never gets to paint at all" (*L*, p. 25).

5. See Brooks, *Toward Yoknapatawpha*, pp. 120–24; and McHaney, "The Elmer Papers," pp. 284–86.

6. At some point Faulkner changed book 3 to book 2; see McHaney, "The Elmer Papers," p. 297.

7. Ibid., p. 283.

8. William Spratling, *File on Spratling: An Autobiography* (Boston: Little, Brown, 1967), pp. 31–33.

9. McHaney, "The Elmer Papers," pp. 282–83, 285, 287–88.

10. Cf. "Elmer" TS, pp. 81–85 and *M*, pp. 335–40.

11. For a comparison of the relevant passages from "Elmer" and *Flags in the Dust*, see Stephen Neal Dennis, "The Making of *Sartoris*: A Description and Discussion of the Manuscript and Composite Typescript of William Faulkner's Third Novel" (Ph.D. diss., Cornell University, 1969), pp. 87–90.

12. See McHaney, "The Elmer Papers," p. 286; and David Minter, *William Faulkner: His Life and Work* (Baltimore: Johns Hopkins University Press, 1980), pp. 56–59. Michael Millgate, *The Achievement of William Faulkner* (London: Constable, 1966), p. 22.

13. "Elmer" TS, p. 47.

14. Brooks, *Toward Yoknapatawpha*, p. 115.

15. James Joyce, *A Portrait of the Artist as a Young Man*, ed. Chester G. Anderson (New York: Viking Press, 1979), pp. 46–47.

16. "Elmer" TS, p. 3.

17. Ibid., p. 4.

18. Joyce, *A Portrait of the Artist*, p. 257.

19. "Elmer" TS, pp. 18, 47, 28, respectively.

20. McHaney, "The Elmer Papers," pp. 295–300.

21. There is, of course, also the unmistakable resemblance to Proust's use of leitmotifs to tie together past and present associations; it is, however, extremely difficult to ascertain at what stage Faulkner became familiar with Proust. On Proust and Faulkner, see Richard P. Adams, "The Apprenticeship of William Faulkner," *Tulane Studies in English* 12 (1962): 137–38; and Michael Millgate, "Faulkner's Masters," *Tulane Studies in English* 23 (1978): 145–46. Also see Arthur F. Kinney, *Faulkner's Narrative Poetics* (Amherst: University of Massachusetts Press, 1973), pp. 60–65.

22. Carvel Collins, Introduction to William Faulkner, *Mayday* (Notre Dame: University of Notre Dame Press, 1978), pp. 3–40; Brooks, *Toward Yoknapatawpha*, pp. 47–52, 59–60.

23. Faulkner, *Mayday*, p. 50.

24. Millgate, *The Achievement of William Faulkner*, p. 75. Collins, Introduction to *Mayday*, pp. 15–23; Brooks, *Toward Yoknapatawpha*, pp. 48–50, 364–66.

25. See Robert Hamblin and Louis Daniel Brodsky, *Selections from the William Faulkner Collection of Louis Daniel Brodsky: A Descriptive Catalogue* (Charlottesville: University Press of Virginia, 1979), p. 22.

26. Faulkner, *Mayday*, p. 56.

27. Ibid., p. 50.

28. See Gail Moore Morrison, "'Time, Tide, and Twilight': *Mayday* and Faulkner's Quest Toward *The Sound and the Fury*," *Mississippi Quarterly* 31 (1978): 351–52.

29. Brooks, *Toward Yoknapatawpha*, pp. 50–51; Collins, Introduction to *Mayday*, pp. 23–35; also see Morrison, "'Time, Tide, and Twilight,'" pp. 347–57. Collins's overelaborate argument hinges on the initial physical position of the figures in relation to Sir Galwyn (at his right and left hand) and their function as instigators of the action. As the tale unfolds, however, little attention is paid to their positions, and rather than "pull and haul Sir Galwyn throughout *Mayday*" as Collins suggests (p. 34), they behave as proper squires, staying "obediently near" their knight. They also remain nebulous and fundamentally indistinguishable, and to see them as representatives of "the hungering Id" and the "painfully punishing Ego" seems extravagant and misleading.

30. Although Carvel Collins suggests that Faulkner began *The Sound and the Fury* while in Europe in 1925, he provides no reliable evidence to support this claim (Introduction to *Mayday*, pp. 24–25). On this point, also see Morrison, "'Time, Tide, and Twilight,'" pp. 338–40.

31. John Faulkner, *My Brother Bill: An Affectionate Reminiscence* (New York: Trident, 1963), p. 155.

32. Blotner, *Faulkner*, 1:490–92, 501–2, 692.

33. "Mistral" seems to have been completed by November 1928; see James B. Meriwether, "Faulkner's Correspondence with *Scribner's Magazine*," in *Proof 3*, ed. Joseph Katz (Columbia: University of South Carolina Press, 1973), p. 256. Also see idem, "The Short Fiction of William Faulkner: A Bibliography," in *Proof 1*, ed. Joseph Katz (Columbia: University of South Carolina Press, 1971), pp. 288, 300, 310; and idem, *Literary Career*, pp. 176–80.

34. See Hans H. Skei, "The Novelist as Short Story Writer" (Ph.D. diss., University of Oslo, 1980), pp. 58–59.

35. Dated typescript in the Faulkner Collection, Alderman Library, University of Virginia.

36. For the relationship to *Crome Yellow*, see Edwin T. Arnold, "Faulkner and Huxley: A Note on *Mosquitoes* and *Crome Yellow*," *Mississippi Quarterly* 30 (1977): 433–36; and M. Gidley, "Some Notes on Faulkner's Reading," *Journal of American Studies* 4 (1970): 92–94. For the relationship to *Those Barren Leaves*, see Oldenburg, "Faulkner's Early Experiments," pp. 177–84. In her 1927 review of *Mosquitoes* (reprinted in, *William Faulkner: The Critical Heritage*, ed. John Bassett [London: Routledge and Kegan Paul, 1975], pp. 66–67), Lillian Hellman appears to have been the first critic to note the resemblances between Faulkner's novel and *Those Barren Leaves*. More recently, Carvel Collins alludes to a 1925 letter in which Faulkner mentioned that he had just read *Those Barren Leaves* ("Biographical Background for Faulkner's *Helen*," in William Faulkner, *Helen: A Courtship and Mississippi*

Poems [New Orleans: Tulane University Press; Oxford, Miss.: Yokna-patawpha Press, 1981], pp. 32–33).

37. The blurb on the novel's dustjacket advertises the resemblance between *Mosquitoes* and Douglas's bestseller—"one is irresistibly re-minded of 'South Wind' by this book"—and a few reviewers subse-quently commented on the comparison. See, for example, Ruth Suckow's review, reprinted in, *William Faulkner: The Critical Heritage*, pp. 69–70.

38. Aldous Huxley, *Those Barren Leaves* (London: Chatto and Win-dus, 1925), p. 58.

39. There has been a good deal of confusion concerning Julius's sur-name. Several critics have assumed that it is "Wiseman," like that of his sister Eva Wiseman, even though it is clear that this is her married name; others have guessed that it is "Kauffman," since Julius, at one point (*M*, p. 327), notes that his grandfather's name was Julius Kauffman; yet this, of course, could very well have been his maternal grandfather. Faulkner never provides Julius with a definite surname, preferring, for whatever reason, to call him "the Semitic man" throughout the novel.

40. Oldenburg, "Faulkner's Early Experiments," pp. 180–83.

41. Willard Huntington Wright, *The Creative Will: Studies in the Phi-losophy and the Syntax of Aesthetics* (New York: John Lane, 1916), p. 210.

42. Aldous Huxley, *Point Counter Point* (London: Chatto and Win-dus, 1928), p. 409.

43. On the question of language in this novel, see John T. Matthews, *The Play of Faulkner's Language* (Ithaca: Cornell University Press, 1982), pp. 45–50.

44. Faulkner may have picked up this anecdote from his friend Sprat-ling; see Brooks, *Toward Yoknapatawpha*, p. 140.

45. See, for example, Keen Butterworth, "A Census of Manuscripts and Typescripts of William Faulkner's Poetry," *Mississippi Quarterly* 26 (1973): item 26, pp. 340–41.

46. Now published in Faulkner, *Uncollected Stories*, pp. 480–88.

47. Compare, for example, the section describing St. Anthony's en-counter with the Queen of Sheba. This book remained one of Faulkner's favorite works of literature; see *FU*, p. 56 and *LG*, pp. 225, 243. Collins notes that in 1925 Faulkner owned a copy of *La Tentation de Saint An-toine* in French ("Background for *Helen*," p. 56).

48. Cf. "Elmer" TS, p. 82.

49. "Elmer" TS, p. 82. The image of the girl with hair "neither brown nor gold" appears in much of Faulkner's early work. See, for example, "New Orleans" (*NO*, p. 14) and "The Kid Learns" (*NO*, p. 91).

50. See, for example, Kenneth William Hepburn, "Faulkner's *Mosquitoes*: A Poetic Turning Point," *Twentieth Century Literature* 17 (1971): 19–28; and Sally R. Page, *Faulkner's Women: Characterization and Meaning* (Deland, Fla.: Everett/Edwards, 1972), pp. 30–32.

51. Millgate, *The Achievement of William Faulkner*, p. 73.

52. Edwin T. Arnold, "Freedom and Stasis in *Mosquitoes*," *Mississippi Quarterly* 28 (1975): 295.

53. See chap. 2, n. 18.

54. Brooks, *Toward Yoknapatawpha*, p. 132.

55. For Faulkner's debt to Joyce, see Joyce W. Warren, "Faulkner's 'Portrait of the Artist,'" *Mississippi Quarterly* 19 (1966): 121–31; Craig Werner, "Beyond Realism and Romanticism: Joyce, Faulkner and the Tradition of the American Novel," *Centennial Review* 23 (1979): 248–52; and André Bleikasten, *The Most Splendid Failure: Faulkner's "The Sound and the Fury"* (Bloomington: Indiana University Press, 1976), pp. 28–32. For his debt to Eliot, see Frederick L. Gwynn, "Faulkner's Prufrock—and Other Observations," *Journal of English and Germanic Philology* 52 (1953): 63–70. For his debt to Hergesheimer, see Phyllis Franklin, "The Influence of Joseph Hergesheimer upon *Mosquitoes*," *Mississippi Quarterly* 22 (1969): 208–13. For his debt to Rostand, see Brooks, *Toward Yoknapatawpha*, p. 139.

56. See Wright, *The Creative Will*, pp. 66–76, 86–87.

57. For a pertinent example of Friend's work, see "The Double Dealer: Career of a 'Little' Magazine," in Leland H. Cox, Jr., ed., "Julius Weis Friend's History of the *Double Dealer*," *Mississippi Quarterly* 31 (1978): 589–604.

58. See Brooks, *Toward Yoknapatawpha*, p. 379, 141–44, 149–50, 378–80, for a general discussion of the people who lie behind the characters in *Mosquitoes*; and Blotner, *Faulkner*, 1:512–22.

59. Bleikasten, *Splendid Failure*, p. 26.

60. Millgate, *The Achievement of William Faulkner*, p. 72.

61. Sherwood Anderson, *The Modern Writer* (San Francisco: Lantern Press, 1925), p. 23.

62. Sherwood Anderson, "A Note on Realism," in his *Sherwood Anderson's Notebook* (New York: Boni and Liveright, 1926), pp. 75–76.

63. Sherwood Anderson, *A Story Teller's Story* (New York: Huebsch, 1924), p. 291.

64. Sherwood Anderson, *Winesburg, Ohio* (New York: Huebsch, 1919), pp. 199–200. Although acutely aware of Anderson's artistic limitations, Faulkner always thought very highly of *Winesburg, Ohio*. See, for example, *NO*, p. 133–34.

65. See Albert J. Guerard, *The Triumph of the Novel: Dickens, Dos-*

toevsky, Faulkner (New York: Oxford University Press, 1976), p. 206.
66. In his review of the novel (reprinted in, *William Faulkner: The Critical Heritage*, p. 64), Conrad Aiken notes: "There is a great deal of talk in the book—so much, that one finds oneself thinking that the thing might almost better have been a play; a farce-comedy. And the talk falls naturally and easily into scenes. One suspects that it would take very little pruning and shaping to turn the thing into an actable affair, with the characters just enough broadened into caricature to make them easily actable."
67. Ibid.

5. Expedition into Regionalism: "Father Abraham" and *Flags in the Dust*

1. During this period Faulkner wrote "The Wishing Tree," a children's fantasy based in part on *Mayday* (see James B. Meriwether, "The Short Fiction of William Faulkner: A Bibliography," in *Proof 1*, ed. Joseph Katz [Columbia: University of South Carolina Press, 1971], pp. 310–11); a soon-to-be-abandoned narrative entitled "The Devil Beats His Wife" (see Meriwether, "The Short Fiction of William Faulkner," pp. 313–14); the introduction and captions for *Sherwood Anderson and Other Famous Creoles: A Gallery of Contemporary New Orleans* (New Orleans: Pelican Bookshop Press, 1926), a collection of caricatures drawn by his friend William Spratling (see Joseph Blotner, *Faulkner: A Biography*, 2 vols. [New York: Random House, 1974], 1:534–35); and completed "Royal Street," a hand-rendered version of "New Orleans" (Noel Polk, "'Hong Li' and *Royal Street*: The New Orleans Sketches in Manuscript," *Mississippi Quarterly* 26 (1973): 294–95). Apparently he also gave *Helen: A Courtship* to Helen Baird at this time (see Carvel Collins, "Biographical Background for Faulkner's *Helen*," in William Faulkner, *Helen: A Courtship and Mississippi Poems* [New Orleans: Tulane University Press; Oxford, Miss.: Yoknapatawpha Press, 1981], p. 12). Stone's notice is quoted in James B. Meriwether, "Sartoris and Snopes: An Early Notice," *Library Chronicle of the University of Texas* 7 (1962): 37.
2. Manuscript, Arents Collection, New York Public Library; the quotation is from p. 4.
3. Emily Whitehurst Stone, "Faulkner Gets Started," *Texas Quarterly* 8 (1965): 143.
4. See, for example, Cleanth Brooks, "Faulkner as Poet," *Southern Literary Journal* 1 (1968): 10; and Martin Kreiswirth, "Faulkner's *The Marble Faun*: Dependence and Independence," *English Studies in Canada* 6 (1980): 335–37.

5. Although this essay was first published in 1925, a typescript, as Joseph Blotner notes, bears the date "October 1924" (Introduction to *Mississippi Poems*, in Faulkner, *Helen: A Courtship*, p. 137).

6. "Mississippi Hills: My Epitaph" was Poem VII of the handmade pamphlet he gave to Myrtle Ramey in 1924 (*Helen: A Courtship*, p. 156); it was revised and reprinted as "My Epitaph," in *Contempo* 1 (1932): 2; and subsequently appeared as Poem XLIV of *GB*, p. 67. Also see Keen Butterworth, "A Census of Manuscripts and Typescripts of William Faulkner's Poetry," *Mississippi Quarterly* 26 (1973): item 41, pp. 344–45.

7. See Cleanth Brooks, *William Faulkner: Toward Yoknapatawpha and Beyond* (New Haven: Yale University Press, 1978), pp. 97–99.

8. Malcolm Cowley, *The Faulkner-Cowley File* (New York: Viking, 1968), p. 109.

9. William Faulkner, *Essays, Speeches, and Public Letters*, ed. James B. Meriwether (New York: Random House, 1965), p. 8.

10. Although there is no firm evidence, it is possible that "A Rose for Emily" was also drafted as a part of this collection—especially since there exists an early Liveright contract for an anthology entitled "A Rose for Emily and Other Stories" (*L*, p. 35).

11. Faulkner, "Trial Preface to *Sartoris*," in Max Putzel, "Faulkner's Trial Preface to *Sartoris*: An Eclectic Text," *Papers of the Bibliographical Society of America* 74 (1980): 374–75.

12. Cowley, *The Faulkner-Cowley File*, p. 66. On the transmutation of the Faulkner clan into fiction, see David Wyatt, *Prodigal Sons: A Study in Authorship and Authority* (Baltimore: Johns Hopkins University Press, 1980), pp. 76–87.

13. Blotner, *Faulkner*, 1:537–38, 545.

14. Joseph Conrad, *Notes on Life and Letters* (London: Dent, 1921), p. 7.

15. Michael Millgate, *Thomas Hardy: His Career as a Novelist* (New York: Random House, 1971), pp. 345–50.

16. See William R. Ferris, "William Faulkner and Phil Stone: An Interview with Emily Stone," *South Atlantic Quarterly* 68 (1969): 540. It is clear that Balzac was from an early date one of Faulkner's favorite authors; see Emily Whitehurst Stone, "How a Writer Finds His Materials," *Harper's*, Nov. 1965, p. 158; and James B. Meriwether, "Early Notices of Faulkner by Phil Stone and Lewis Cochran," *Mississippi Quarterly* 17 (1964): 141. For the relationship between the *Comédie humaine* and Yoknapatawpha, see Roxandra I. Antoniadis, "The Human Comedies of Honoré de Balzac and William Faulkner: Similarities and Differences" (Ph.D. diss., University of Colorado, 1970), pp. 7–46.

17. D. Starke, *Character: How to Strengthen It*, trans. Lorenzo O'Rourke (New York: Funk and Wagnalls, 1915), pp. 111–12; see Joseph Blotner, comp., *William Faulkner's Library: A Catalogue* (Charlottesville: University Press of Virginia, 1964), p. 118. In "Fouqué's *Undine* and Edith Wharton's *The Custom of the Country*," *Revue de littérature comparée* 45 (1971): 181, Thomas L. McHaney notes that the presentation of Flem's economic rise might also owe something to the description of Elmer Moffatt in *The Custom of the Country*. Moffatt "simply appeared one day behind the counter" of a local store and went on to edge his way into the powerhouse of the town's water works.

18. See Michael Millgate, *The Achievement of William Faulkner* (London: Constable, 1966), p. 24.

19. Blotner, *Faulkner*, 1:559–60.

20. Stephen Neal Dennis, "The Making of Sartoris: A Description and Discussion of the Manuscript and Composite Typescript of William Faulkner's Third Novel" (Ph.D. diss., Cornell University, 1969), p. 68.

21. Faulkner, "Trial Preface," p. 376.

22. For a discussion of the reliability of the Random House text of *Flags in the Dust* and the extent to which it represents (as the editor of the novel, Douglas Day, says in his introduction, p. ix) "a faithful reproduction" of the typescript in the Faulkner Collection, Alderman Library, University of Virginia, see Richard P. Adams, "At Long Last *Flags in the Dust*," *Southern Review* 10 (1974): 878–88; George F. Hayhoe, "William Faulkner's *Flags in the Dust*," *Mississippi Quarterly* 28 (1975): 370–86; and the lively exchange between Thomas L. McHaney and Albert Erskine in the *Faulkner Concordance Newsletter* 2 (Nov. 1973): 7–8, and 3 (May 1974): 2–4.

23. See, for example, Dennis, "Making of *Sartoris*," and James E. Kibler, review of Dennis's "Making of *Sartoris*," *Mississippi Quarterly* 24 (1971): 315–19, which challenges Dennis's central hypothesis and provides a less complex and more probable alternative; Melvin Reed Roberts, "Faulkner's *Flags in the Dust* and *Sartoris*: A Comparative Study of the Typescript and the Originally Published Novel" (Ph.D. diss., University of Texas at Austin, 1974); Merle Wallace Keiser, "*Flags in the Dust* and *Sartoris*," in *Fifty Years of Yoknapatawpha: Faulkner and Yoknapatawpha 1979*, ed. Doreen Fowler and Ann J. Abadie (Jackson: University Press of Mississippi, 1980), pp. 44–70; and n. 22 above.

24. Faulkner, "Trial Preface," p. 376.

25. Blotner, *Faulkner*, 1:560.

26. Warren Beck, *Faulkner: Essays* (Madison: University of Wisconsin Press, 1976), p. 177.

27. Millgate, *The Achievement of William Faulkner*, pp. 84–85.

28. Brooks, *Toward Yoknapatawpha*, p. 391.

29. Faulkner, "Trial Preface," p. 376.

30. See, for example, George Marion O'Donnell, "Faulkner's Mythology," *Kenyon Review* 1(1939): 285–99; Malcolm Cowley, introduction to his edition of *The Portable Faulkner* (New York: Viking Press, 1946), pp. 1–24; and Cleanth Brooks, *William Faulkner: The Yoknapatawpha Country* (New Haven: Yale University Press, 1963), passim.

31. On onomastic repetition, see, for example, Ingeborg Bachmann, "Über 'Schall und Wahn,'" in *Über William Faulkner*, ed. Gerd Haffmans (Zurich: Diogenes, 1973), pp. 127–29; Nathalie Sarraute, *The Age of Suspicion*, trans. Maria Jolas (New York: George Braziller, 1963), pp. 69–71; and Jonathan Culler, *Structuralist Poetics: Structuralism, Linguistics, and the Study of Literature* (Ithaca: Cornell University Press, 1975), pp. 23–38; Olga Vickery, *The Novels of William Faulkner: A Critical Interpretation*, rev. ed. (Baton Rouge: Louisiana State University Press, 1964), pp. 19–20; and John Irwin, *Doubling and Incest/Repetition and Revenge: A Speculative Reading of Faulkner* (Baltimore: Johns Hopkins University Press, 1975), pp. 64–66.

32. According to Faulkner the aviators in particular "had exhausted themselves psychically . . . they were unfitted for the world that they found afterward" (*FU*, p. 23).

33. T. H. Adamowski, "Bayard Sartoris: Mourning and Melancholia," *Literature and Psychology* 23 (1973): 149–58; also see Ralph Page, "John Sartoris: Friend or Foe?" *Arizona Quarterly* 23 (1967): 27–33.

34. Michael Millgate, "Faulkner's Masters," *Tulane Studies in English* 23 (1978): 148.

35. Hugh Wiley, *The Wildcat* (New York: Doran, [1920]). Faulkner alludes to this novel in a letter to his mother, postmarked September 22, 1925 (*L*, p. 23). In *Selected Letters* (*L*, p. 25) and *Faulkner*, 1:192, Blotner mistakenly calls it *The Military Wildcat* and provides neither the author's name nor any bibliographical information.

36. Richard T. Dillon, "Some Sources for Faulkner's Version of the First Air War," *American Literature* 44 (1973): 629–37.

37. Faulkner, *Essays, Speeches, and Public Letters*, p. 197.

38. For a discussion of Bayard as a Gothic hero, see Elizabeth M. Kerr, *William Faulkner's Gothic Domain* (Port Washington, N.Y.: Kennikat Press, 1979), pp. 78–79; and Dieter Meindl, *Bewusstsein als Schicksal: Zu Struktur und Entwicklung von William Faulkners Generationenromanen* (Stuttgart: Metzler, 1974), pp. 90–100.

39. H. Edward Richardson, *William Faulkner: The Journey to Self-Discovery* (Columbia: University of Missouri Press, 1969), pp. 171, 227–28.

40. Millgate, *The Achievement of William Faulkner*, p. 76.

41. André Bleikasten, *The Most Splendid Failure: Faulkner's "The Sound and the Fury"* (Bloomington: Indiana University Press, 1976), p. 36.

42. Ibid., p. 39.

43. See chap. 4, n. 11 above.

44. In his idiosyncratic, but interesting, chapter on Faulkner in *Men without Art* (London: Cassells, 1934), pp. 46–48, Wyndham Lewis sees these repetitions as showing how little regard Faulkner had for *le mot juste*.

45. Although in *The Triumph of the Novel: Dickens, Dostoevsky, Faulkner* (New York: Oxford University Press, 1976), pp. 220–21, Albert J. Guerard sees the passage on the mule as marking Faulkner's stylistic "self-discovery," it seems more closely allied to the kind of deliberate verbal experiments (for example, the italicized dream fantasy in *Mosquitoes*) that appeared in earlier works.

46. William Faulkner, *Sartoris* (New York: Random House, 1956), p. 2. On the relevance of this opening for the novel's theme of "necrolatry," see André Bleikasten, "Fathers in Faulkner," in *The Fictional Father: Lacanian Readings of the Text*, ed. Robert Con Davis (Amherst: University of Massachusetts Press, 1981), pp. 122–25.

47. For an even earlier opening, see William Faulkner, "The Rejected Manuscript Opening of *Flags in the Dust*," ed. George F. Hayhoe, *Mississippi Quarterly* 33 (1980): 371–83.

48. Bleikasten, *Splendid Failure*, p. 41.

49. See Kerry McSweeney, "The Subjective Intensities of Faulkner's *Flags in the Dust*," *Canadian Review of American Studies* 8 (1977): 157–58; and William Cosgrove, "The 'Soundless Moiling' of Bayard Sartoris," *Arizona Quarterly* 35 (1979): 165–69.

6. Quitting Reading: *The Sound and the Fury*

1. William Faulkner, "An Introduction for *The Sound and the Fury*," ed. James B. Meriwether, *Southern Review* 8 (1972): 709.

2. William Faulkner, "An Introduction to *The Sound and the Fury*," ed. James B. Meriwether, *Mississippi Quarterly* 26 (1973): 412–13. Although written at about the same time, this version of the introduction is substantially different from the one published in the *Southern Review*,

and subsequent references to it will read "An Introduction to *The Sound and the Fury*" (*MQ*).

3. Sherwood Anderson, *A Story Teller's Story* (New York: Huebsch, 1924), p. 94.

4. William Faulkner, *Faulkner at West Point*, ed. Joseph L. Fant and Robert Ashley (New York: Vintage, 1969), p. 81.

5. Faulkner, "An Introduction for *The Sound and the Fury*," p. 710.

6. Faulkner, "An Introduction to *The Sound and the Fury*" (*MQ*), p. 412.

7. Faulkner, "An Introduction for *The Sound and the Fury*," pp. 708, 710.

8. On the psychocreative importance of this figure for the composition of *The Sound and the Fury*, see André Bleikasten, *The Most Splendid Failure: Faulkner's "The Sound and the Fury"* (Bloomington: Indiana University Press, 1976), pp. 51–57.

9. Bleikasten, *Splendid Failure*, p. 5; also see pp. 1–2 in text.

10. Irving Howe, *William Faulkner: A Critical Study*, 3d ed. (Chicago: University of Chicago Press, 1975), pp. 20–21.

11. Lawrence Lipking, *The Life of the Poet: Beginning and Ending Poetic Careers* (Chicago: University of Chicago Press, 1981), p. 16.

12. See Charles D. Peavy, "The Eyes of Innocence: Faulkner's 'The Kingdom of God,'" *Papers on Language and Literature* 2 (1966): 178–82; Edward M. Holmes, *Faulkner's Twice-Told Tales: His Re-Use of His Material* (The Hague: Mouton, 1966), pp. 106, 113; and Carvel Collins, Introduction to *NO*, p. xxviii.

13. For Benjy's diction, see L. Moffitt Cecil, "A Rhetoric for Benjy," *Southern Literary Journal* 3 (1970): 32–46, especially 38–42. For his sentence structure, see Irena Kaluza, *The Functioning of Sentence Structure in the Stream-of-Consciousness Technique of William Faulkner's "The Sound and the Fury": A Study in Linguistic Stylistics* (Philadelphia: Folcroft Press, 1970), pp. 43–50; also see Richard Gunter, review of Kaluza, *Mississippi Quarterly* 22 (1969): 264–79, for the limitations (notably, its use of the unreliable English edition of the text) of this otherwise excellent study, as well as for Gunter's own pertinent comments. For Benjy's sense of time, see Perrin Lowrey, "Concepts of Time in *The Sound and the Fury*," in *English Institute Essays, 1952*, ed. Alan S. Downer (New York: Columbia University Press, 1954), pp. 57–82, especially 67–70; and Bleikasten, *Splendid Failure*, pp. 76–78.

14. For the debt to Sir Galwyn, see Carvel Collins, Introduction to William Faulkner, *Mayday* (Notre Dame: University of Notre Dame Press, 1978), pp. 27–28; Gail Moore Morrison, "'Time, Tide, and Twilight':

Mayday and Faulkner's Quest Toward *The Sound and the Fury*," *Missis-sippi Quarterly* 31 (1978): 345–57; David Minter, *William Faulkner: His Life and Work* (Baltimore: Johns Hopkins University Press, 1980), pp. 62–63, 85–86; and chap. 4, n. 29 above. For the debt to Horace Benbow, see Melvin Backman, "Faulkner's Sick Heroes: Bayard Sarto-ris and Quentin Compson," *Modern Fiction Studies* 2 (1956): 100; and Robert M. Slabey, "The 'Romanticism' of *The Sound and the Fury*," *Mississippi Quarterly* 16 (1963): 151.

15. *Chronophobia* is Bleikasten's term for Quentin's pathological ob-session with time (*Splendid Failure*, p. 127).

16. See Max Putzel, "Evolution of Two Characters in Faulkner's Early and Unpublished Fiction," *Southern Literary Journal* 5 (1973): 60–61; and chap. 4, n. 12.

17. Faulkner had previously used a "cracked and stained" slipper in association with Patricia Robyn (*M*, p. 235).

18. "Elmer" typescript, Faulkner Collection, Alderman Library, Uni-versity of Virginia, p. 30.

19. See Douglas B. Hill, Jr., "Faulkner's Caddy," *Canadian Review of American Studies* 7 (1976): 26–38; Bleikasten, *Splendid Failure*, pp. 65–66; and Linda W. Wagner, "Language and Act: Caddy Compson," *Southern Literary Journal* 14 (1982): 49–61.

20. In *Sartoris* (New York: Random House, 1956), p. 289, the same sentence ends: ". . . into silence again, leaving no ripple, in the still darkness."

21. See, for example, Faulkner, "An Introduction for *The Sound and the Fury*," p. 710.

22. Ibid., p. 708.

23. This description also contributes to the "images of obliquity" that recur throughout Quentin's section. See John W. Hunt, *William Faulk-ner: Art in Theological Tension* (Syracuse, N.Y.: Syracuse University Press, 1965), pp. 62–66.

24. Bleikasten, *Splendid Failure*, pp. 60–62, 100–102.

25. See pp. 74–75 in the text.

26. The identification of the two men is implied early in the mono-logue (*SF*, p. 113) when Quentin's thoughts move directly from Bland to Ames.

27. Ford Madox Ford, *Joseph Conrad: A Personal Remembrance* (London: Duckworth, 1924), p. 173.

28. Edward W. Said, *Beginnings: Intention and Method* (New York: Basic Books, 1975), especially pp. 29–40, 81–101.

29. In "The Irrelevant Detail and the Emergence of Form," in *Aspects*

of Narrative: Selected Papers from the English Institute, ed. J. Hillis Miller (New York: Columbia University Press, 1971), p. 82, Martin Price states: "The openings of novels serve to set the rules of the game to be played by the reader. The degree of specification in setting, the presence or absence of a persona behind the narrative voice, the verbal density of the style—its metaphorical elaboration or cultivated innocence—all these are ways of indicating the nature of the game, of educating the responses and guiding the collaboration of the reader." On the formal and rhetorical aspects of opening strategies, also see Victor Brombert, "Opening Signals in Narrative," *New Literary History* 11 (1980): 489–502; Steven Kellman, "Grand Openings and Plain: The Poetics of First Lines," *Sub-Stance* 17 (1977): 139–47; Meir Sternberg, *Expositional Modes and Temporal Ordering in Fiction* (Baltimore: Johns Hopkins University Press, 1978) especially chap. 1; and Ian Watt, "The First Paragraph of *The Ambassadors*: An Explication," *Essays in Criticism* 10 (1960): 250–74.

30. In *Lectures on Russian Literature*, ed. Fredson Bowers (New York: Harcourt Brace Jovanovich, 1981), p. 255, Vladimir Nabokov said this of Chekhov.

31. In the original text, "One said" is followed by a period. I have changed the period to a comma in accordance with Meriwether's "suggested correction." See James B. Meriwether, "Notes on the Textual History of *The Sound and the Fury*," *Papers of the Bibliographical Society of America* 56 (1962): 302.

32. For a linguistic analysis of Benjy's "mind style," see Geoffrey N. Leech and Michael H. Short, *Style in Fiction: A Linguistic Introduction to English Fictional Prose* (London: Longman, 1981), pp. 202–7.

33. Bleikasten, *Splendid Failure*, p. 88.

34. See Lawrence E. Bowling, "Faulkner: Technique of *The Sound and the Fury*," *Kenyon Review* 10 (1948): 552–66; and Isadore Traschen, "The Tragic Form of *The Sound and the Fury*," *Southern Review* 12 (1976): 799–802.

35. In *Splendid Failure*, p. 51, Bleikasten uses the term *empty center* to explain Caddy's role in the psychocreative processes of the book's composition; I use it to describe a narrative strategy. Also see *Splendid Failure*, pp. 65–66; John T. Matthews, *The Play of Faulkner's Language* (Ithaca: Cornell University Press, 1982), pp. 20–21; and David Williams, *Faulkner's Women: The Myth and the Muse* (Montreal: McGill-Queens University Press, 1977), pp. 64–65.

36. Faulkner, *Faulkner at West Point*, p. 111.

37. Cleanth Brooks, "Faulkner's First Novel," *Southern Review* 6

(1970); 1062; also see Bleikasten, *Splendid Failure*, pp. 19–20.

38. Bleikasten, *Splendid Failure*, p. 65.

39. From 1931 onward Faulkner included *The Nigger of the "Narcissus"* in practically every list of his favorite books. See, for example, *LG*, pp. 17, 21, 60; and *FU*, pp. 144, 150.

40. Joseph Conrad, *The Nigger of the "Narcissus"* (New York: Doubleday, Doran, 1933), p. 14.

41. See, for example, Jacques Derrida, "Structure, Sign and Play in the Discourse of the Human Sciences," in his *Writing and Difference*, trans. Alan Bass (Chicago: University of Chicago Press, 1978), pp. 278–93.

42. On the question of absence in the novel, see Matthews, *The Play of Faulkner's Language*, pp. 63–114.

43. See John Irwin, *Doubling and Incest/Repetition and Revenge: A Speculative Reading of Faulkner* (Baltimore: Johns Hopkins University Press, 1975), pp. 55–56.

44. Faulkner states that Benjy "was not even aware that Caddy was missing. He knew only that something was wrong, which left a vacuum in which he grieved. He tried to fill that vacuum" (*LG*, p. 246).

45. In *Flags in the Dust*, Bayard and John, of course, also lose their father when they are very young. In "Elmer," all of the Hodge children leave home prematurely largely because of the deficiencies of their parents.

46. See Albert J. Guerard, *The Triumph of the Novel: Dickens, Dostoevsky, Faulkner* (New York: Oxford University Press, 1976), pp. 112, 117–18; and Irwin, *Doubling and Incest*, p. 160. On incest in *The Sound and the Fury*, see Bleikasten, *Splendid Failure*, pp. 78–80, 96–97, 114–16; and Irwin, *Doubling and Incest*, pp. 43–53.

47. For the autobiographical roots of this familial configuration, see Judith Wittenberg, *Faulkner: The Transfiguration of Biography* (Lincoln: University of Nebraska Press, 1979), pp. 75–82. Also see John Earl Bassett, "Family Conflict in *The Sound and the Fury*," *Studies in American Fiction* 9 (1981): 1–20.

48. William Faulkner, *Go Down, Moses, and Other Stories* (New York: Random House, 1942), pp. 130–31.

49. For a discussion of the psychological implications of Quentin's problem, see Charles D. Peavy, "'If I Just Had a Mother': Faulkner's Quentin Compson," *Literature and Psychology* 23 (1973): 114–21; and M. D. Farber, "Faulkner's *The Sound and the Fury*: Object Relations and Narrative Structure," *American Imago* 34 (1977): 327–50. In his introduction to *"The Sound and the Fury": A Concordance to the Novel*, ed. Noel Polk and Kenneth L. Privratsky (Faulkner Concordance Advis-

ory Board, 1980), 1:x, André Bleikasten points out that the word *mother* is the most frequently used noun in the novel (excluding proper names). On Mr. Compson's role as a father, see André Bleikasten, "Fathers in Faulkner," in *The Fictional Father: Lacanian Readings of the Text*, ed. Robert Con Davis (Amherst: University of Massachusetts Press, 1981), pp. 115–22, 125–29; idem, *Splendid Failure*, pp. 109–14; and Irwin, *Doubling and Incest*, pp. 67–69, 110–13.

50. While Dilsey, of course, shows sympathy and compassion and literally holds the family together, her age, position in the household, and, especially, her race, keep her from becoming a true maternal surrogate. See Lee C. Jenkins, *Faulkner and Black-White Relations: A Psychoanalytic Approach* (New York: Columbia University Press, 1981), pp. 161–76.

51. See Irwin, *Doubling and Incest*, pp. 43–53; and Bleikasten, *Splendid Failure*, pp. 78–80, 96–97, 114–16.

52. Richard P. Adams, *Faulkner: Myth and Motion* (Princeton: Princeton University Press, 1968), pp. 39–40; Edmond L. Volpe, *A Reader's Guide to William Faulkner* (New York: Farrar, Straus, 1964), p. 56; John T. Frederick, "Anticipation and Achievement in Faulkner's *Soldiers' Pay*," *Arizona Quarterly* 23 (1967): 244; Hyatt H. Waggoner, *William Faulkner: From Jefferson to the World* (Lexington: University of Kentucky Press, 1966), pp. 4–5; and Bleikasten, *Splendid Failure*, p. 237.

53. For Faulkner's knowledge of actual black sermons, see Bruce A. Rosenberg, "The Oral Quality of Rev. Shegog's Sermon in William Faulkner's *The Sound and the Fury*," *Literatur in Wissenschaft und Unterricht* 2 (1969): 73–88. For discussions of the Easter service, see Adams, *Myth and Motion*, pp. 226–30; Bleikasten, *Splendid Failure*, pp. 195–20; Gabriel Vahanian, *Wait without Idols* (New York: George Braziller, 1964), pp. 111–15; and Amos N. Wilder, "Vestigial Moralities in *The Sound and the Fury*," in *Religious Perspectives in Faulkner's Fiction: Yoknapatawpha and Beyond*, ed. J. Robert Barth, S.J. (Notre Dame: University of Notre Dame Press, 1972), pp. 91–102.

54. See Victor Strandberg, "Faulkner's Poor Parson and the Technique of Inversion," *Sewanee Review* 73 (1965): 181–90.

55. On the question of the novel's closure, see John V. Hagopian, "Nihilism in Faulkner's *The Sound and the Fury*," *Modern Fiction Studies* 8 (1967): 45–55; Beverly Gross, "Form and Fulfillment in *The Sound and the Fury*," *Modern Language Quarterly* 29 (1968): 439–49; Bleikasten, *Splendid Failure*, pp. 186–206; M. Ted Steege, "Dilsey's Negation of Nihilism: Meaning in *The Sound and the Fury*," *Washington State University Research Studies* 38 (1970): 266–75; and Walter J. Sla-

toff, *Quest for Failure: A Study of William Faulkner* (Ithaca, N.Y.: Cornell University Press, 1960), pp. 155–58.

56. See Hagopian, "Nihilism in Faulkner's *The Sound and the Fury*," pp. 50–51; and Bleikasten, *Splendid Failure*, pp. 183–84, 238.

57. On "retrospective patterning" and literary form, see Barbara Hernnstein Smith, *Poetic Closure: A Study of How Poems End* (Chicago: University of Chicago Press, 1968), pp. 10–14. On the problem of narrative closure in general, see, for example, Frank Kermode, *The Sense of an Ending: Studies in the Theory of Fiction* (London: Oxford University Press, 1966), especially chaps. 5 and 6; the special issue of *Nineteenth-Century Fiction* 33 (1978) on narrative endings; David H. Richter, *Fable's End: Completeness and Closure in Rhetorical Fiction* (Chicago: University of Chicago Press, 1974); Marianna Torgovnick, *Closure in the Novel* (Princeton: Princeton University Press, 1981); and D. A. Miller, *Narrative and Its Discontents: Problems of Closure in the Traditional Novel* (Princeton: Princeton University Press, 1981).

58. Henry James, Preface to *Roderick Hudson*; reprinted in, *The Art of the Novel: Critical Prefaces*, ed. R. P. Blackmur (New York: Scribners, 1953), p. 6. On "closural allusions," see Smith, *Poetic Closure*, pp. 172–82.

59. For other intertextual "presences," see, for example, John M. Howell, "Hemingway and Fitzgerald in *The Sound and the Fury*," *Papers on Language and Literature* 2 (1966): 234–42; Thomas L. McHaney, "Robinson Jeffers' 'Tamar' and *The Sound and the Fury*," *Mississippi Quarterly* 22 (1969): 261–63; James M. Mellard, "Caliban as Prospero: Benjy and *The Sound and the Fury*," *Novel* 3 (1970): 233–48; also see Joseph Brogunier, "A Housman Source in *The Sound and the Fury*," *Modern Fiction Studies* 18 (1972): 220–25; Ida Fasel, "A 'Conversation' between Faulkner and Eliot," *Mississippi Quarterly* 20 (1967): 195; Philip M. Weinstein, "Caddy Disparue: Exploring an Episode Common to Proust and Faulkner," *Comparative Literature Studies* 14 (1977): 38–52; and Jean Weisgerber, *Faulkner and Dostoevsky: Influence and Confluence* (Athens: Ohio University Press, 1974), pp. 179–92.

60. On Joyce's influence, see Richard P. Adams, "The Apprenticeship of William Faulkner," *Tulane Studies in English* 12 (1962): 139–40; Michael Millgate, "Faulkner's Masters," *Tulane Studies in English* 23 (1978): 146–49; Michael Groden, "Criticism in New Composition: *Ulysses* and *The Sound and the Fury*," *Twentieth-Century Literature* 21 (1975): 265–77; Carvel Collins, "The Interior Monologues of *The Sound and the Fury*," in *English Institute Essays, 1952*, ed. Alan S. Downer

(New York: Columbia University Press, 1954), pp. 29–56; Robert Humphrey, *Stream of Consciousness in the Modern Novel* (Berkeley and Los Angeles: University of California Press, 1965), pp. 16–20, 68–70, 104–11; Robert Martin Adams, *Afterjoyce: Studies in Fiction after "Ulysses"* (New York: Oxford University Press, 1977), pp. 82–88; and Hugh Kenner, "Faulkner and Joyce," in *Faulkner, Modernism, and Film*, ed. Evans Harrington and Ann J. Abadie (Jackson: University Press of Mississippi, 1979), pp. 20–33. Also see William R. Ferris, "William Faulkner and Phil Stone: An Interview with Emily Stone," *South Atlantic Quarterly* 68 (1969): 541–42.

61. Willard Huntington Wright, *The Creative Will: Studies in the Philosophy and the Syntax of Aesthetics* (New York: John Lane, 1916), pp. 182–83.

62. Faulkner, "An Introduction for *The Sound and the Fury*," p. 708, and Faulkner, "An Introduction to *The Sound and the Fury*" (*MQ*), p. 414.

63. Faulkner, "An Introduction for *The Sound and the Fury*," p. 708.

64. In "An Introduction to *The Sound and the Fury*" (*MQ*), Faulkner speaks of James and replaces Dostoyevsky with Turgenev (p. 414). For an interesting psychoanalytic analysis of this process of creative maturation, see Meredith Skura, "Creativity: Transgressing the Limits of Consciousness," *Daedalus* 109 (1980): 127–46, especially 133–34.

65. Faulkner, "An Introduction for *The Sound and the Fury*," p. 709.

Index

"Verse Old and Nascent: A
  Pilgrimage," 102
"Victory," 80
Vision in Spring, 11

Wasson, Ben, 110–12
The Waste Land (Eliot), 53, 91
"Wealthy Jew" ("New Orleans"),
  25–26, 79, 88
Wessex: and Yoknapatawpha,
  106–7
Wharton, Edith, 176 (n. 17)
"What Is Wrong with Marriage,"
  37
The Wildcat (Wiley), 118
The Wild Palms, 72–73

Wiley, Hugh, 118
Winesburg, Ohio (Anderson), 93,
  103
"The Wishing Tree," 174 (n. 1)
Woolf, Virginia, 56, 96, 140
Wright, Austin McGiffert, 161
  (n. 1)
Wright, Willard Huntington, 4–6,
  7, 10, 14, 15, 16, 17, 18, 23–
  24, 27, 35, 37, 50, 69, 84, 92,
  103, 153, 154

Yoknapatawpha: founding of,
  101–9, 111–17
Yonce, Margaret, 166 (n. 8)